PROOF
of
ANGELS

THE DEFINITIVE BOOK ON
THE REALITY OF ANGELS AND
THE SURPRISING ROLE THEY
PLAY IN EACH OF OUR LIVES

Ptolemy Tompkins and Tyler Beddoes

Foreword by Colleen Hughes

HOWARD BOOKS
AN IMPRINT OF SIMON & SCHUSTER, INC.

NEW YORK · NASHVILLE · LONDON · TORONTO · SYDNEY · NEW DELHI

HOWARD BOOKS

An Imprint of Simon & Schuster, Inc.
1230 Avenue of the Americas
New York, NY 10020

First Howard Books trade paperback edition February 2016

HOWARD and colophon are trademarks of Simon & Schuster, Inc.

For information about special discounts for bulk purchases, please contact Simon & Schuster Special Sales at 1-866-506-1949 or business@simonandschuster.com.

The Simon & Schuster Speakers Bureau can bring authors to your live event. For more information or to book an event, contact the Simon & Schuster Speakers Bureau at 1-866-248-3049 or visit our website at www.simonspeakers.com.

Interior design by Dana Sloan

Manufactured in the United States of America

10 9 8 7 6 5 4 3

Library of Congress Cataloging-in-Publication Data

Names: Tompkins, Ptolemy.
Title: Proof of angels : the definitive book on the reality of angels and the surprising role they play in each of our lives / Ptolemy Tompkins and Tyler Beddoes.
Description: First [edition]. | Nashville : Howard Books, 2016.
Identifiers: LCCN 2015039720
Subjects: LCSH: Angels—Christianity.
Classification: LCC BT966.3 .T66 2016 | DDC 202/.15—dc23
LC record available at http://lccn.loc.gov/2015039720

ISBN 978-1-5011-2918-6 (hardcover)
ISBN 978-1-5011-2922-3 (paperback)
ISBN 978-1-5011-2920-9 (ebook)

For Jennifer Lynn Groesbeck

Contents

Foreword

ONE OF THE biggest events in my years as editor of *Angels on Earth* magazine came in the summer of 1999, when an applicant for a position that had opened at *Guideposts* and *Angels on Earth* came in for an interview. *Angels* and *Guideposts* are in the same offices. Edward Grinnan, the editor in chief of *Guideposts*, thought it would be a good idea if I took a look at the potential hire.

As we talked—me explaining what *Guideposts* and *Angels* were about, and Ptolemy telling me about his interests and work up to that point in his life—I noticed that his eye kept traveling to my bookshelves. My office had a lot of shelf space, much of it taken up with books on angels, but plenty of it empty.

It wasn't long before I was going over to Ptolemy's office and giving him stories to work on. At our offices someone is always on the phone, talking to the narrator of a story, asking questions, and making suggestions for how to shape and structure it. I soon got used to hearing Ptolemy's voice in his office doing just that.

At first Ptolemy worked on the usual *Angels* story—a first-person narrative that the editor works to create with the person who has had an angelic experience. But before too long, he branched out. He started producing what we call "thought pieces" for me: articles that would take a subject that at first glance seemed to have little to do with angels, and show how this wasn't the case at all. I loved these articles, and began to feature them as cover stories every other issue. From seeds to seashells to birds to stars, wherever Ptolemy turned his gaze he seemed to find connections with angels. The shelves of his office overflowed with books, and I realized what he must have been thinking that day we met in my office: *Why aren't all of her shelves completely full?*

In 2007 Ptolemy left *Guideposts* and *Angels* to work on a book called *The Divine Life of Animals*, the idea for which had come from an article he'd written for *Guideposts* about animals and the afterlife. The article turned out to be one of the most popular in the magazine's history, and Ptolemy spent the next year developing and enlarging the idea.

Today, Ptolemy and I are married. Though he no longer works in our offices, in a way not much has changed. He still has too many books on his shelves downstairs in his study, and during the time he spent working with Dr. Eben Alexander on *Proof of Heaven* and *The Map of Heaven*, I'd often hear Ptolemy on the phone, shaping the narrative, bouncing ideas back and forth, just as he would have done had it been a *Guideposts* or *Angels on Earth* story. In fact, Ptolemy called *Proof of Heaven* his "ultimate *Guideposts* story," and though the result was not a *Guideposts* article but a bestselling book, I could see why he felt that that was just what it was.

One morning last March, I sent Ptolemy a link to a story that we'd discussed in the weekly editorial meeting: a story about a young woman who had crashed in a river, and the police officers who had worked to save her, believing she was alive because of a voice that came from inside the car. It was just the kind of story Ptolemy would have liked: tragic, mysterious, but also deeply hopeful. I knew that *Angels on Earth* readers wouldn't have taken that mysterious voice for anything other than the voice of an angel, and I knew that Ptolemy would have loved bringing out the details and drama of the story to maximum effect.

Could we do the story justice in our pages, or was it too big a story, too bittersweet, for our short format? I sent Ptolemy the link.

An hour or so later, Ptolemy called. Not too long after my email had come in, he'd received a call from an agent working with one of the police officers who had been on hand at the crash. The agent—Jennifer Gates—knew Ptolemy's work, and thought he might be able to turn the story into a book. She even had a title in mind: *Proof of Angels*.

For the next few months, our house was more like an extension of the *Guideposts* and *Angels on Earth* offices than ever before. Ptolemy and police officer Tyler Beddoes were on the phone constantly, developing not just a working relationship but what I soon realized was a deep friendship as well. Ptolemy believed that just as *Proof of Heaven* was his "ultimate *Guideposts* story," *Proof of Angels* was going to be his ultimate *Angels on Earth* story.

Reading it now, I have to agree. And I can't help but think that an angel might have been at work that morning Ptolemy received not just an email from me about Tyler's story, but a call from Jennifer as well.

—Colleen Hughes, editor of
Angels on Earth magazine

PROOF
of
ANGELS

Introduction

"Don't try to prove anything."
—ELISABETH KÜBLER-ROSS

A FEW YEARS AGO, I took my stepdaughter Evie snorkeling for the first time. She was eight, and though she'd put a face mask on before, she'd never had a chance to look below the waves in an area that was really populated with sea life. We were in the Bahamas, floating in the water by what looked like a pretty humdrum chunk of rock. Evie pushed and fumbled at her mask, getting the water out of it and blowing through her snorkel so she could breathe. When she was finally comfortable with her equipment, she lowered her head beneath the water.

Kaboom. The reef was swarming with fish—parrot fish, triggerfish, and swarms of little black-and-yellow sergeant majors that were all around her, investigating her completely without her knowledge. I'll never forget the look in her

1

eyes when she brought her head back out of the water and the uncontrollable smile that formed around the snorkel in her mouth. She had thought she was just bobbing about by a barren rock, when in fact she had been immersed in a whole other universe of color and light and life.

Imagine: the world, changed in an instant from a place of fear and uncertainty and emptiness to a place of wonder and beauty and overwhelming numbers of beings, invisible but present all the same.

Imagine a helmet like the ones old-fashioned divers used to wear: one that covers the entire head like a fishbowl. Then imagine that this helmet is made of a magical, glass-like substance, one so thin and unobtrusive that it lets just about everything through. It never gets dirty, never gets wet, and is absolutely transparent to light and penetrable by air. Essentially, it's as if this helmet isn't there at all.

Except it is. And the one thing this helmet blocks out—the one thing it keeps the person wearing it from experiencing—is the spiritual world. Everything else gets past these helmets. But that one thing—that singular, all-important part of the world, without which the world isn't really the full, complete world at all, but only half of it—doesn't make it through.

Sometimes, if the light and the circumstances are just right, you can catch a glimpse of the helmets on the heads of other people as they pass by you in the street. Sometimes the helmets other people wear are so obvious—so completely visible—that it seems laughable that they themselves could fail to notice that they're wearing them. But then, just as often, most of us fail to notice that we ourselves are wearing one.

What kind of a world do we see when looking through these magical, spirit-filtering helmets? We see a world in which the earth is just the earth, where good things and bad things happen, where there is happiness and sorrow, where people are born and people die. Yet somehow, none of this seems to mean all that much. We see a world in which everything is relative and essentially insignificant, but complaining about this fact, or even bringing it up, seems silly.

Along with having no real purpose, the world seen through the glass of this helmet has no real justice either. Some people do "good" things, and others do "bad" things, but these are really just words we have cooked up to try to make sense of things that we actually can't make any sense of. Bad people often do very well in this strange, pointless world, while nice ones have to bear up under all manner of pressures and struggles.

One of the strangest things about these helmets is that, even when we become aware that we're wearing them, we can't simply take them off. They can't be wrenched off with our arms or shattered with a sledgehammer. They are extremely stubborn, extremely resilient.

At least, they are most of the time. But sometimes moments come along when these helmets seem to disappear all by themselves, with no effort on our part at all. Suddenly they are just . . . gone. In moments like this, we find ourselves looking around at the world as if we'd never seen it before.

Those moments are what this book is about.

For ten years I worked at a magazine called *Angels on Earth*, the sister publication of *Guideposts*, a magazine featuring inspirational stories that was founded in 1949 by Norman Vincent Peale. A product spawned by the modern boom in interest in angels, *Angels on Earth* tells stories of actual angelic encounters and (because believable versions of these are not exactly a dime a dozen) stories of ordinary, everyday people who act in an angelic fashion. I quickly took to my work there and was fascinated to see just how little I knew about the lore of angels—how many there are, how few are actually mentioned in the Old or New Testaments, and how much thought the truly great minds of philosophy and religion have devoted to them.

Early on at the magazine, while casting about for good subjects for stories, I encountered a book called *My Descent into Death* by a painter, art instructor, and vocal nonbeliever named Howard Storm. While on a vacation in Paris with his wife, Storm suffered a perforated duodenum that nearly killed him. Lying in his hospital bed, he suddenly found himself feeling light, vital, and better than he could recall feeling in a long, long time, if ever.

Storm got to his feet, and—like many an NDE-er before him—was shocked to see a wizened, pathetic figure lying in the bed he'd just gotten up from: a figure that, he was dumbfounded to realize, was himself (or rather, his physical body). Storm then noticed voices out in the hall, gently beckoning him to follow. Wandering into the hall, Storm found himself surrounded by strange, small creatures. At first they seemed friendly, but gradually Storm realized they weren't. The beings began to mock him, prod him, and even bite him. Scared out of his wits, Storm cried out for help to a God whom, up to then, he had never addressed, formally or otherwise, because he'd had no belief in him.

His prayer was immediately answered. Storm found himself rising up into a world of light, life, beauty, and a love so overpowering that it blasted the old, unbelieving Storm to pieces. Love, Storm discovered, was not the gooey sentiment, the pretty, empty thing that he had thought it was. Instead, it turned out that this most ephemeral of subjects was the real material—the real *substantia* (Latin, "that which stands beneath")—that is the true foundation of everything in our world. It is the genuine stuff that this world is made of, the single absolutely irreducible source of all that we see and feel and think and are. There is nothing it cannot stand up to, because there is nothing more elemental than it is. Ironically enough, it is the real, ultimate, unbreakable atom that the scientists of the late nineteenth and early twentieth centuries were looking for with such confidence and enthusiasm. Love, that flimsy sentiment, turned out to be the one substance that they could not burn or crush or flay or otherwise defile. In a world where everything could be caught, held down, and examined by science, love was the one substance that was not to be so treated—the one thing that always got away.

When Storm recovered from his ordeal he was so different from the intelligent but crotchety and embittered man he'd been before that for his wife it was as if he had been replaced by another person. And, in a sense, he had been.

But what interested me most in Storm's book was a short

and rather comical scene that occurred when he was back in America. Storm, still in very rickety shape, decided he wanted to attend church. With essentially no experience of this practice, he picked one from the directory in his local newspaper. Storm writes:

I picked one based on the information that it met in a public school. This indicated to me that this church was not materialistic, since it didn't own property. God would surely be present in a nonmaterialistic church.

On Sunday morning, with much effort, I got cleaned up and dressed in suit and tie and off we went to a church fifteen miles away.

Storm arrived to find that, to his great disappointment, the church was closed for the summer. But not long afterward, Storm's friend told him of a church just a mile from his home that might fit the bill. The following Sunday, Storm, still in very poor shape, arrived at the church. He walked up the steps, leaning heavily on his wife.

What a pitiful sight I must have been to the greeters at the door of the church. Emaciated, jaundiced skin, yellow eyes, leaning on my wife, dragging my feet up the steps.

The worship had just begun with the congregation singing the opening hymn when we entered the sanctuary. A few feet inside, I saw on the ceiling of the church hundreds of angels basking in praise of God. They were a golden color and radiated golden light around them.

The unexpected sight of the angels unleashed powerful
emotions of awe of God from inside me. I did the only
thing I could do in that circumstance, which was to throw
myself down on the floor. Prostrate on the carpeted aisle, I
thanked God and praised God profusely.

Regrettably, we were not in a Pentecostal church,
where this might have been acceptable behavior. My wife
bent over me, concerned that I had collapsed. The ushers
rushed to her aid, asking if they should call an ambulance.
Then my wife realized that I was in religious ecstasy and
became furious with me because of the commotion I was
creating in the back of the church. She was yelling in
my ear, "Get up! Get up! We will never come to church
again!"

I originally read Storm's book in its first edition by Floris
Books, before Anne Rice discovered it and helped it become a
best seller, and I like to think his appearance in *Angels on Earth*
got his name out to a few more readers. When I interviewed
Storm for *Angels on Earth*, he struck me as completely earnest
but curiously subdued—curiously quiet. There did not seem
to be much in the way of ego at work in him.

I felt the same way when I spoke to Natalie Sudman, an
employee of the Army Corps of Engineers in Basra and Na-
siriyah in Iraq. Natalie was blown up by a roadside bomb
while riding in a military vehicle. Sudman was severely injured in the blast—so severely that, reading her book *Appli-*
cation of Impossible Things, I couldn't help but be impressed
that someone who had suffered such terrifying, brutal physi-

cal pain could speak not only with forgiveness but also with genuine gratitude for her experience.

The blast immediately transferred Sudman into what she called the "blink environment," so named because everything that happened did so within the time it takes an eye to blink. In other words, the blast exploded Sudman not only out of her body, but also out of ordinary, linear time as we experience it on earth.

How do you describe what it's like to be outside time? You can't, but that doesn't stop Sudman from taking her best shot at it all the same. Immediately upon leaving her body, Sudman found herself speaking with a vast crowd of beings—beings whom she somehow recognized even though she had never, to her knowledge, given a thought to the existence of dimensions outside time, much less the possibility of beings who could live there. For Sudman, the world changed in an instant. You could call it the "instant of the angel."

The details in both Storm's and Sudman's books are fascinating, but what makes me mention them here is not their fantastic stories, but simply the way these two people sounded when I talked to them. Both these people had remarked straight-out in their books that they had conversed with what we can legitimately call angels. And doing so, I couldn't help but feel, had unplugged something in them: that urgent desire to *matter* on an earthly level that both I, and most of the people I know, spend so much of our time worrying about. Sudman, in particular, simply did not seem interested in fame, attention, or what people thought of her. How could such a thing be?

Here, from French reporter Pierre Jovanovic's remarkable book *An Inquiry into the Existence of Guardian Angels*, is an example of an angelophany all the more believable for the unusual nature of the specifics that surrounded it. It is told by a man who as a youth had been in the Yugoslav army in 1956.

One afternoon following a very long march . . . I grew dizzy, my chest tightened and my legs grew heavy. I couldn't walk. They had to take me on a stretcher to the barracks, where the doctor auscultated me and rushed me to the Domzale military hospital in Ljubljana. There the doctors diagnosed a heart fibrillation. I was in critical condition. I remember a sinister emergency room which I shared with an old colonel in no better shape than I was. Despite the tons of medicine they made me swallow, I felt no better; on the contrary. After a month in the hospital I felt myself weakening faster and faster. One night I opened my eyes suddenly, and to my great surprise two sublime girls stood before me in almost sparkling white robes. Before I go on, I should specify that these were not hospital nurses. Nurses in Yugoslavian hospitals, and military hospitals especially, bore no resemblance to models. . . . [The girls] seemed to exist in a kind of fog, and I don't know how to explain that. But at the same time I could distinguish them clearly. So I wanted to see them closer up. . . . And inexplicably I had the feeling that strength was invading me, enough for me to rise out of the bed and approach them. . . . But once I was on my feet, I saw no one in the room. That lasted no more than ten or fifteen seconds. I didn't understand all this too well, and thirty-seven years later I still think about it often. The fact remains that my health started to improve, and a month and a half later I left the hospital. During the last days I remember surprising two doctors who were murmuring together, saying, "Tough luck for this boy. So young, and he hasn't long to live." And indeed I've had some cardiac problems since because of my feeble constitution. But I've survived, and I tell myself that if they are what I will meet after death, I have nothing to fear.

One of the things I like about this story is precisely the detail that would make many a reader suspicious of it. The soldier telling the tale hardly makes a secret of the first thing he noticed about the two angels who came to visit him: they were cute. Had he met them under different circumstances, he might have asked one of them out.

That's what's so great. This man, likable as he is in his tough way, is not the sort to believe in angels. He has seen something, we can believe, of the pain of the world, and he is most decidedly a realist. Therefore, when he tells us of the strange realness of these women who visited him, we are inclined to believe him. Angels were clearly not the first thing on this man's mind as he lay in that grim Yugoslav hospital. Yet they are what he saw.

These are the voices I like. They are, precisely, voices that are not naive. And when someone who is not naive, who knows very, very well that this world is not a land of sweetness and sunshine, encounters an angel, it's hard not to be impressed. When someone who is the last person in the world to think he's going to see something *sees it anyhow*, it delivers a certain kind of satisfaction that few other kinds of stories can give.

It's precisely because he is not the "angel type" that this soldier's story is so interesting—if we are ready to let down our guard and actually pay attention to what he is saying. And if we are truly interested in the question of whether or not angels exist, that is exactly what we have to do.

Right here, in our world of arguments and violence, where no one agrees with anyone, and the clutter and noise of that disagreement drives all of us ever deeper into distraction and despair, there exists the possibility of an encounter that flattens all of that instantly, that makes all the dead, dull, gray, picayune bickering between believers of one sort and believers of another sort, and between believers and nonbelievers, blow away like so much straw.

I had the same kind of reaction when I was introduced, by phone, to Tyler Beddoes, a young Utah police officer who, while quite different in character from the Yugoslav soldier, was also a wonderfully unlikely individual to have an angelic experience. Tyler did not see an angel, much less two angels, in white robes. In fact, he didn't even see an angel at all. But he heard one, and if I had still worked at *Angels on Earth* when I heard his story, I would have gone over to the office of Colleen Hughes, the editor in chief of *Angels*, and told her about it. Tyler's story, the minute I heard it, brought me back to the kind of zone I would fall into when working on a really good

Angels on Earth story: I would get this funny feeling of surprise that somehow or other, my life had led me to this place where I had the opportunity to talk to person after person who had had a brush with the miraculous. Colleen emailed me the story about Tyler early one morning, right after it broke, and I was still thinking of it later in the day when I got a call from an agent I knew, asking if I'd like to do a book on it.

I didn't have to think very long.

The closest I myself have come to seeing an angel happened on September 11, 2001. I was in New York City, standing on the corner of Fifth Avenue and Twelfth Street, looking up at Tower One of the World Trade Center, when it essentially seemed to liquefy and collapse. (Tower Two, of course, fell first, but I had not seen it fall, and with all the dust in the air, I thought it was still standing. And after all, who on earth would ever dream that one of those towers would fall to begin with?)

Why was that moment the closest I have come to seeing an angel? Because that moment did for me what many an encounter with an angel has done for other people. It showed me in a single instant that the world is not the solid, substantial place I had been taught to think it was, but a much more precarious one. A world made, in essence, out of ash. If the solid world is *that* un-solid, *that* ephemeral, what hope is there?

Once you see just how unbearably, terrifyingly unstable the physical world really is, you are ready, you are open to discover its deeper architecture.

The physical world is the definition of insubstantiality. To discover that, get sick. To discover that, pick up the phone and find out that someone you love has been in an automobile accident, or a plane crash, or a school shooting. Today the scientific search for the solid is at an end. There *is* nothing solid, nothing enduring, nothing that's going to stick around. Nothing lasts, nothing remains. All is sand. You can't count on anything. You can't lean on anything.

That is the origin of the wonderful solidity of the angel. The angel is an introduction to the fact that where the solid world we thought we lived in ends, another world begins. Just at that moment when there is nothing, or worse than nothing, a new world reveals itself out of the mist and settling dust of the old one. Just as the last pillar of the old world falls, the dim outlines of the new world appear. This new world is an *actual* world. It is not a world of phantoms and ghosts, but a world of reality and truth and the most solid, enduring architecture we can imagine.

The world seems to cheat us by teaching us to love people or animals and then taking them away. Lean on the world, and the world will break. That was brought home to me that day when I saw Tower One fall. I had the tremendous privilege of seeing what I had thought of as the epitome of solidity reveal itself as . . . nothing. When that tower fell before my eyes, it fell with the shocking swiftness of a curtain dropping. And beyond that curtain was the true, naked reality of what kind of place the world really is.

But the story doesn't end there. One overcast evening the following September, I was walking my dog in the same Greenwich Village neighborhood I'd been in when I'd seen Tower One fall. To memorialize the World Trade Center buildings and the people who had died in them, two extremely powerful lights had been set up at the spot where the towers had stood: lights so powerful that, shining straight up into the night, they punctured easily through the layers of cloud covering the city.

The vision of those powerful lights punching up through the ascending levels of cloud cover created a strange effect. It was as if the beams of light were revealing level after level of the inside of a vast, multistoried building, one with complex goings-on within each floor, and floor after floor stretching far up into the sky. The heavens were showing themselves to be what Jacob saw on the night of his dream in Genesis: a structure of many stories, with beings moving constantly up and down them.

This, in essence, is the two-part education that angels give us. They demonstrate that the world we think we live in—the world of refrigerators and automobiles and school lunches and jobs and retirement parties—is nothing more than an evanescent cloud: a bunch of nothing that looks like something but really isn't. But beyond that world of nothing-that-looks-like-something, there is a world where exactly the opposite is the case: a world that (from our blinkered perspective) doesn't seem to exist at all, but where the true solidity we so crave is really to be found.

Angels tell us that behind the illusory world of the everyday, there lurks not simply *nothing*, not a terrible aching void, such as the one that so many people of unsure faith today struggle so hard not to think about, but another, *deeper* architecture. That realm of deeper architecture is where the angel comes from and where it returns when it is done visiting us. *This*, and no other, is the real and lasting world.

"From a certain point on," the enigmatic writer Franz Kafka famously wrote, "there is no more turning back. That is the point that must be reached."

That point, that definitive, all-changing moment, is the subject of this book.

CHAPTER 1

***

An Occurrence on Spanish Fork Bridge

Ten years ago I had what could only be described as a nervous breakdown. I was thirty-three and depressed. I was afraid of dying and all the other symptoms of this illness. I was alone one day and a voice spoke to me. The voice came from within but was clear and distinct. It simply said, "Carry on as you are and you are dead." From that moment I started to get better and grew strong in mind and body. I feel a new person. I find I am able to help others with similar problems. The strange thing is though I have not heard the voice since, I feel that something or someone is watching over me and having a large influence on my thoughts and life. I also have this very strong feeling that we, mankind that is, are a part of something far beyond my comprehension. My life has new meaning and purpose.

—SEEING THE INVISIBLE

IN SEPTEMBER OF 1776, two Franciscan friars searching for a route from Santa Fe to Monterey, California, happened to stop at a spot in northern Utah where a canyon met up with a small river. This little confluence of canyon and river eventually began to go by the name of Spanish Fork.

By the middle of the nineteenth century, when the influx of Mormons into Utah was in full swing, Spanish Fork had become a town in earnest—a small but solid "X" on the map of potential destinations for Mormon pioneers from the Eastern states or outside the country (Spanish Fork still has a particularly high number of Mormon immigrants with Icelandic blood).

Today, Spanish Fork is a town of some forty thousand people with a reasonably good economy (thanks in large part to Provo, home of Brigham Young University, where many of its residents work) and which hovers, like a thousand other towns like it across the country, somewhere between the old America and the new. Last spring, a Walmart opened on U.S. Route 6 outside town, consigning to doom the already teetering Kmart that had killed off a good portion of the downtown's older businesses when it itself went up in the late eighties. On Main Street and its cross streets, the mishmash of shops with local Western character that hung on till the early eighties has now been replaced by the mini-mall shop fronts you see in every town across America. There's a Verizon store, a Sonic drive-in, a Taco Bell, and (proof that the town has truly made the jump from then to now) a Starbucks.

Main Street runs north to south through town. Then, without changing its name, it leaves its stores and gas stations behind and gives way to flat farm country, fields of wheat and corn and alfalfa punctuated by an occasional clutch of houses: landscape that hasn't changed for decades. To the east, the Wasatch Mountains stand as they have for millions of years, their particularly hard, granular snow drawing thousands of skiers to the area every winter.

About a mile outside town, Main Street crosses the Spanish Fork River, the source of the town's name but now little more than an unassuming, domesticated runoff that empties into Utah Lake some ten miles farther west. Before white settlers arrived and drove them out, a nomadic Native American tribe known as the Ute, or "fish eaters," used to camp on the river's banks in the summer months to take advantage of the plentiful fish that crowded its waters, and which, though in much smaller numbers, still lure fishermen to its banks. The first Western-style house went up in Spanish Fork in 1850, and the last of the Ute were driven out by the late 1880s, when Mormon settlers were pouring into the area in their greatest numbers, following Brigham Young's resolution to take the religion given to Joseph Smith by the angel Moroni to the virgin lands of the West.

The new arrivals set to turning Spanish Fork into the place it remains today: a small, friendly town, still largely Mormon but (sins against the Ute committed in the previous century notwithstanding) amicable to members of other faiths as well. The town is a genuine community, built in the spirit that America was founded on: faith in a common God, expressed in different ways.

Narrow (about fifteen feet at its widest point) and sluggish save for the spring months when it comes to life with runoff from the Wasatch Mountains, the Spanish Fork River captured media attention only once, in 1983, when it briefly made headlines across the country after a massive spring landslide caused by excessively heavy rains sealed it off some ten miles upriver from Spanish Fork, just below the little town of Thistle. Foreshadowing the kinds of water disasters that are regular business in the West these days, a lake formed from the backed-up water, deep enough to drown out Thistle and kill it permanently. It took two weeks and two million dollars before a tunnel could be bored through the sludge and mud and the river set to flowing again, making it at the time the nation's costliest water disaster on record.

At around 10:00 p.m. on Friday, March 6, 2015, Jennifer Lynn Groesbeck was driving her 2009 red Dodge Caliber home from dinner with her dad in Salem, a town some five miles south of Spanish Fork, to her home in Springville, a town to the northeast situated about halfway between the mountains to the east and Provo Bay to the north. Traveling on Main Street at or close to the speed limit of 45 miles per hour, Jennifer veered inexplicably to the right just before reaching the Spanish Fork Bridge and went into the river.

The car left the road with a strange and tragic accuracy. Had Jennifer swerved just a foot or two earlier, she would have struck a small stand of trees: trees that were big enough to stop her car but small enough, and with enough give in their trunks, that they most likely would have brought it to a halt gently enough not to harm anyone inside. Likewise, had Jennifer traveled just a few feet farther before swerving, the right side of her car would have struck the graduated divider that runs the length of the bridge. In that situation, too, her car most likely would have ground to a halt before going into the river.

But Jennifer went off the road right between those two barriers. When her car swerved, her right front wheel missed the graduated divider, while her left front wheel caught its edge and rode up it, causing the car to flip as it sailed over the water. It landed upside down with brutal force in the shallows three-quarters of the way across the river, blowing out the windshield and bringing the roof down like a mousetrap on Jennifer's upper body, killing her instantly.

Unlikely and unlucky as Jennifer's crash into the river was, people who knew her were quick to say that Jenny Lynn had no reason to end her life. She was young and well liked, and she was enrolled at Provo College in the medical assistant program. She also had a new baby: eighteen-month-old Lily, who was in the car with her the night of the crash and whose unlikely survival (not only of the crash itself but also of the long hours before the car's discovery) was soon to become news all around the world.

Unseen and unnoticed, the car sat as it had landed in the river for the next fourteen hours, the 45-degree water entering through the shattered upstream passenger's side window and flowing back out the driver's side, accommodating with ease and indifference to the new obstacle in its path. Behind Jenny, still strapped snugly in the car seat in which Jenny had placed her less than half an hour earlier, Lily lay suspended upside down in the dark, some twelve inches above the flowing water, which for the remainder of the night and into the first several hours of daylight drifted past beneath her like the gently moving cloud-scape of an upside-down sky.

Jenny had dressed Lily in tights, a leopard-print jumpsuit, and a pink sweatshirt for the chilly early spring evening. Against all odds, her clothes remained dry during the crash—a crucial factor in keeping her alive through the night. Had her clothes been splashed with water from the river in the impact, or had the car landed just a few feet shorter in a deeper section of the river or at a slightly different angle, or had her car seat been improperly secured, or had a thousand other small details differed from what did happen, Lily would have gone the way of her mother. But all things worked in her favor. Even the cold temperature of the water played a part, for by cooling the air in the car, it most likely keyed Lily's metabolism to slow down to conserve her body's heat. At eighteen months Lily also still had her full layer of baby fat, which combined with the clothing Jennifer had dressed her in to seal her off from the chilly, 55-degree night around her. She was a lucky baby.

Four cops were on duty in Spanish Fork that March Saturday, in charge of keeping the peace among the town's forty thousand inhabitants. Though Spanish Fork has its share of petty thefts, marital squabbles, public drunkenness, and the other mild but manageable mishaps of any town its size, Saturdays tend to be slow. One of those on-duty cops was Tyler Beddoes, then twenty-nine years old and a ten-year veteran of the Spanish Fork Police Department. At about eleven, Tyler's wife, Brittany, called and asked if he wanted to meet her and their kids—Gunnar, three, and Gracie, nine—for his lunch hour at Zupas, a soup-and-salad chain at a mini-mall a few blocks east of Main Street, right next to where the Starbucks had recently gone up. Tyler told her he'd see her there at noon.

Tyler was about halfway through his Nuts-About-Berries salad when his handset went off. A fisherman had called in a report of an abandoned car under the Spanish Fork Bridge.

Seconds later, another voice came over the radio. "This is 6J18. I'll take it."

That was Bryan DeWitt, another of the four officers on duty that day. With DeWitt heading over to check the scene out, Tyler wasn't obligated to respond. But as officer in charge that Saturday, Tyler figured he'd better go, too. He knew the water under the bridge was about five feet deep that time of year, moving fast and cold with runoff from the mountains. DeWitt might need help. Tyler apologized to Brittany and the kids and pressed the speaker button on his shoulder mike. "This is 6J16. I'm en route as well."

Tyler switched on his lights and siren. Driving over, he started thinking on what a strange place the bridge at Spanish Fork was for an abandoned car to end up. If the car hadn't just gone off the road but had been there for a while, why had no one phoned it in earlier? Main Street was a well-traveled road, even out there at the edge of town, and there were several houses not too far from the bridge that would surely have been within earshot of the crash.

In the midst of these thoughts, Tyler's radio went off again. "Officers responding to Spanish Fork Bridge: the caller now says he sees what looks like a hand sticking out of the car." Tyler pushed the accelerator down.

Pulling up just before the bridge and leaving his lights

going, Tyler stumbled down the steep, rocky embankment to the water, where he could see DeWitt peering into the crushed mess of the driver's side window, trying to make sense of what was inside. Tyler joined him and saw the pale, bruised arm of what appeared to be a young woman. It wasn't moving.

The Spanish Fork Police Force had just recently been outfitted with body cams, and on the drive over Tyler had switched his on. Unfortunately, still fairly new to the equipment, he failed to push the switch the full way, and as a result his camera recorded nothing of what happened in the river that morning. DeWitt's camera, however, was working, as was Jared Warner's, who, along with Officer Jason Harward, arrived just seconds behind Tyler. DeWitt's video footage, the longest and the most detailed, records what happened next.

"What do you got?" Warner says as he enters the water and joins the other two.

"Looks like there's two of them," Tyler responds. And to Tyler, staring into the upside-down wreck of the car, it does indeed look, from the splay of limbs visible through the crushed frame of the driver's side window, as if there might be two, not one, persons in the front seat. Breathing hard from adrenaline and the shock of the freezing water, the men move back and forth around the car, trying to figure out the best way to right it. Meanwhile, the voice of a police dispatcher can be heard on the officers' radios, laconically discussing the need for more traffic control at a nearby intersection.

"We don't need any help for traffic control," DeWitt finally responds, exasperated. "A car's in the river."

By now more support vehicles have pulled up on the bridge

overhead, and responders are making preparations to right the car mechanically. "Where's the winch at?" someone asks up above, and we get a brief glimpse of the back of Tyler's head as he peers into the car, still trying to figure out, from the incoherent mess of limbs inside, how many people are in there. Warner shouts, "Here, get over here, Beddoes"—a comment that Tyler later told me "wasn't rude or nothing. The adrenaline just really starts going in a situation like that." The officers all crowd over to the driver's side, and the men ready themselves to heave against the vehicle.

It is just then, at exactly two minutes into DeWitt's body cam video footage, that another sound can be heard. It sounds unmistakably like a human voice. It is high and female, but what it says is indecipherable, at least on the video.

"We're helping, we're coming," Warner responds, emotion in his voice. A car that until then had contained at least one body, most likely deceased, has now become, for these officers, a car containing life. Galvanized, the men crowd up against the car, and DeWitt's body cam image dissolves into a red blur as the men heave mightily, pushing the car up onto its side.

Incredibly, given that they are pushing a 3,189-pound car with at least one passenger that is also half-full of water, they succeed in getting the vehicle propped up onto its right side. But unknowingly, in doing so they have plunged Lily, still in the back and still strapped in her car seat, fully into the lightning cold river she had managed, for the previous fourteen hours, to evade.

Just under half a minute later, at 2:26 on the video, Officer DeWitt says, "We gotta keep going with it if we can." He has, of course, no idea just how right he is. The men, all of them up to their chests in the foaming water, continue to maneuver around the car, shouting into it, encouraging whoever called out for help to hold on. Finally, after a full two minutes, we catch another glimpse of Tyler's head as he again peers into the rear of the car.

"Oh God," he says. "There's a baby."

By this point firemen have arrived, and one of them pulls open the rear passenger door, now pointing skyward, and sinks down into the car. We hear him call for a knife or pair of scissors to cut the straps of the car seat, and a moment later Lily emerges, stiff but apparently alive. The fireman passes her to Tyler, who in turn passes her to Warner, who, with body cam still running, scrambles breathlessly up the incline and hands her to a waiting paramedic. Warner and his camera ride with Lily to the hospital, and we watch as Warner and other emergency workers delicately peel Lily free of her freezing clothes, gently massage her tiny rib cage, and insert a short tube down her trachea to get her breath going. The ambulance arrives at the hospital, Warner rushes her inside, and we watch from his still-running camera as she vanishes into an operating room.

Meanwhile back at the river, Harward's camera, which was also on hand to capture the mysterious voice and DeWitt's response, records the action as the remaining officers and firemen push the car upright. There is, after all, still someone alive in the vehicle. The officers know as much, because they all heard her.

With a final groan from the officers and firemen, the car heaves back onto its tires, and Jenny's body at last comes fully into view. Though we don't see her face on camera, it is clear that the sight is devastating. The impact of the ceiling has crushed the back of her head completely, all but decapitating her, and re- moved the skin from her face right down the middle. While the left side of her face is more or less intact, the right side lies like a mask against her shoulder. She is the only person in the car, and she is very clearly dead.

With the main drama over, the officers' adrenaline levels begin to drop. Slowly shifting their attention from the car to themselves, they become aware of their own condition, their own discomfort. Moving in and out of view of Harward's body cam, Tyler staggers out of the water and up the incline to where Brittany, who has since driven over, is waiting with a change of clothes. Rubbing the back of his head, Tyler notes dazedly that he's cut himself back there somewhere and that his leg, too, is bleeding. An EMT tells him he's hypothermic, wraps him in a blanket, and loads him into the back of an ambulance to take him to the hospital.

"It's funny," Tyler told me later about that ride to the hos- pital. "I was going a mile a minute when we were in the river, but once I got in that ambulance, my mood just plummeted. I knew we'd saved the baby—at least for the moment. I saw her eyelids flutter just a little as I passed her up out of the car, so I knew she was still alive. But somehow I didn't think she'd make it. Especially after that last two-minute dunk she'd gotten in the water because of us. And I couldn't get the way her mom looked out of my head. Her face was so destroyed. I've seen plenty of dead people, but for some reason it was just a real blow to see her like that. I had been so sure she was alive. I don't know. It just brought me down real hard."

As to why he had been "so sure" Jenny was alive, Tyler pushed that question out of his head for the moment.

Tyler was released from the hospital one hour later, and Brittany drove him back to the bridge to pick up his squad car. Tyler found Harward, who hadn't gotten hypothermia and had stayed at the scene the whole time over at the north side of the bridge, finishing up the initial report of the incident. He'd sketched the accident scene and filled out forms, giving the basic details of the event: forms that Tyler knew by heart from filling them out himself thousands of times. Soon DeWitt joined them. Released from the hospital, he'd also decided to make his way back to the scene of the accident. In the way officers do after something big has happened, they gathered together where Harward was finishing his forms.

"Normally," Tyler told me, "this would be the point where you'd start talking with the other officers, getting their idea on what happened and just kind of going over it, kicking it around. Stuff happens so fast. When you bounce it around with the other officers later, you get a clearer picture in your head. That's especially true when something really upsetting has happened. It just kind of helps."

But this time, all four officers were strangely silent. Down below, a county truck was hauling the wreck of Jennifer's car from the water. While Tyler had been at the hospital, firemen had pried Jennifer's body loose from the wreckage with a Jaws of Life set, and she lay, barefoot but still in her shorts and T-shirt, most of her body and all of her face covered by a tarp to protect her from gawkers or photographers on the bridge above.

Looking down at the flinty green water, Tyler found a question forming in his head. It was, he realized, a question that had already been there, in the back of his mind, on the ride to the hospital. It was a crazy question—one that, he knew, he'd probably be best off not asking, because if he got the wrong answer from the other officers, he figured they'd think he'd gone crazy.

At length, he asked it anyhow.

"When you guys were down there in the water," he said, "did you all hear a voice?" For a moment no one said anything, and the question hung there awkwardly in the air above the river.

Then Harward spoke. "Yeah, I heard it."

"Me too," said DeWitt.

"So did I," said Warner.

CHAPTER 2

———∞———

What Are Angels?

They, looking back, all the eastern side beheld
Of Paradise, so late their happy seat,
Waved over by that flaming brand, the gate
With dreadful faces thronged and fiery arms:
Some natural tears they dropped, but wiped them soon;
The world was all before them, where to choose
Their place of rest, and Providence their guide:
They hand in hand with wandering steps and slow,
Through Eden took their solitary way.

—JOHN MILTON, *PARADISE LOST*

ANGELS HAVE ALWAYS been difficult to write about, for many
different reasons. In the past, people knew that the chief reason they were hard to write about was because the subject was
intimidating. There were, it was known, all kinds of angels,
all sorts of cosmic-spiritual levels on which they dwelt, and a
million mysteries attached to these levels, which were so high,
so rarefied, and so mighty from our pathetic earthly perspec-

tive that to say anything on the topic seemed the height of arrogance.

In the Christian tradition, only the great geniuses—Saint Augustine, Saint Thomas Aquinas, Meister Eckhart—would dare go near the subject. The same is the case in literature. Goethe, the greatest German writer of all time, could write about angels. Dante, the greatest Italian poet, could write about them, though he did so always with enormous humility. Milton, the greatest poet in the English language, could write of them, and indeed, they were one of his chief topics.

In short, if you were a giant, you could dare to approach the subject. Otherwise, it was wisest to stay quiet and listen to what other voices had to say on the topic.

Generally speaking, if you wish to address the modern secular world about the possibility that angels might actually be real, you will immediately be dismissed as crazy, naive, or both.

Today, though the topic remains just as challenging to write about, the reasons are quite different. Generally speaking, if you wish to address the modern secular world about the possibility that angels might actually be real, you will immediately be dismissed as crazy, naive, or both. If you want to address the question from within the Christian, Jewish, or Islamic tradition (all three of which have always taken the existence of angels completely for granted), you will often still have trouble. This is because the sheer volume of thought produced by all these traditions over the centuries is such that you will scarcely be able to utter a word before discovering you've said something that the other faith traditions take issue with.

Angels are, in short, an impossible subject.

And yet, somewhat paradoxically, books that take angels seriously are wildly popular. The trendiness of angels with the public at large waxes and wanes, but in our time, the big surge of interest in angels began in the early 1990s. Suddenly these beings, which previously had shown up now and then in movies and TV but mostly on cards at Christmas and disappeared for the rest of the year, were everywhere.

There is something about angels that makes it impossible for people to forget about them for too long.

Why was this? The short answer is that there is something about angels that makes it impossible for people to forget about them for too long. There may be phases during which they sink out of sight, yet those phases always end eventually, and the figure of the angel reemerges, interpreted through the lens of the time in which they have appeared back into the light of human interest.

In 1923, the Austrian poet Rainer Maria Rilke famously wrote, "Every angel is terrifying." What did he mean by this? Essentially, that leaving the human world behind and genuinely seeking to encounter the spiritual world was a vaster, scarier, and more dizzying project than most people think. Angels, for

Rilke, were real, but they were *so* real that their reality threatened to overwhelm us if we approached them in a light and disrespectful way.

But during the angel resurgence that began in the '90s, that idea seemed to have vanished, leaving in its wake a plethora of cute, cuddly, completely harmless angels, eager to do our bidding and make our lives better in a thousand ways, from comforting us when we were lonely to finding us good parking spaces.

This trend of making angels seem like friendly, entirely cozy, and nonthreatening beings was taken by some Christian groups—notably Catholics and Evangelicals—as evidence that people were using angels as stand-ins for a God they either didn't believe in or felt too distanced and alienated from to engage with directly. Some went so far as to suggest that these warm, comforting beings were creations of Satan, designed to lure us ever further away from the true God.

So where, amid these arguments, do real angels lie—if, that is, we are ready to face the inevitable ridicule and grief we will get from one party or another just by using *real* and *angels* in the same sentence?

His countenance was like lightning, and his raiment white as snow: And for fear of him the keepers did shake, and became as dead men. And the angel answered and said unto the women, Fear not ye: for I know that ye seek Jesus, which was crucified. He is not here: for he is risen, as he said. Come, see the place where the Lord lay. And go quickly, and tell his disciples that he is risen from the dead;

*and, behold, he goeth before you into Galilee; there shall ye
see him: lo, I have told you."*

—MATTHEW 28, KING JAMES VERSION

In the earliest episodes of the Hebrew Bible, angels appear
as more or less ordinary people, usually men, who have about
them an indefinable but noticeable aspect of otherworldliness.
The great twentieth-century Russian Christian philosopher
Nicholas Berdyaev wrote that "the spirits of the angelic and the
demoniac hierarchies are not personalistic in the sense in which
the human world and God are personalistic," which means he
recognized that while angels (and demons) are real spiritual beings, *they are not human*. Because of this, we make a mistake in
attributing fully human qualities to them, just as we do when
we treat animals as furry people rather than beings genuinely
different from us. Berdyaev was a great animal lover, and this
does not mean that angels don't, in Berdyaev's view, possess personalities. It simply means that the personalities they possess are
something other than the kind we possess. Angels are different
kinds of beings from you and I, and it is therefore a (sometimes
dangerous) mistake to give them specifically human attributes.

Angels were not portrayed with wings, generally, until the
fourth century AD, probably because biblical writers were anxious to separate them from the numerous winged deities and
demons worshipped by the peoples around them. (The classic "angel" we think of today owes a great deal to the famous
winged statue of Nike, the goddess of victory: a piece of Greek
art, but one of such power that it made an indelible impression
on the Christians who saw it.)

*Angels—if you listen to the stories that
people tell about them—can be dressed in
white robes or three-piece suits. What makes
them angels is not what they wear but the
fact that they are spiritual beings who break
into our world to tell us something.*

A helpful definition to remember when trying to sort out just how "genuine" angels differ from the numerous winged beings that populated all sorts of ancient mythologies is this: they are manifestations from above who appear here in the world below, where by nature they don't belong, but which they visit, on occasion, because of the benefit they can provide to certain individuals who need assistance.

Angels—if you listen to the stories that people tell about them—can be dressed in white robes or three-piece suits. What makes them angels is not what they wear but the fact that they are spiritual beings who break into our world to tell us something. Beyond the questions surrounding the guises that angels assume when they appear in our world, there lies a larger and more fundamental one: Do angels always mean us good, or are they capable of meaning us evil? Both evil angels and good ones appear in the New Testament, and orthodox Christianity takes as a matter of course that both types are real: not allegorical but actual spiritual beings, capable of both appearing to and taking up house within the psyches of individual people. All angels can see infinitely more of us than we can see of them—

a generalization with which the great geniuses of angelology agree. Angels are smart. Generalizing further, we can say that the good angels want to assist us in our process of growing toward the beings God wants us to be, and the evil ones are dead set on subverting this process, because, as members of the fallen third of the heavenly host, they don't approve of our existence to begin with.

The word angel *comes, via old French, from the Greek* angelos, *or messenger. Angels are messengers from God.*

In most cases, when a good angel appears, the force of the encounter is such that the people who experience it have no doubt of the goodness of the being that has come before them. But again, because angels are not familiar earthly beings, but transearthly emissaries of extreme power and a certain irreducible "otherness," that intuition of goodness also often comes with a good deal of surprise or even shock. Angels are not beings of earth but of a "somewhere else": one that lies above the earth (not in the simple geographical sense, of course, for angelic reality transcends the three-dimensional existence in which we are, for the moment, situated, and by whose rules we have to communicate), and when they appear here, they rock the bearings of the world in a way we are not used to. When angels come to the rescue of people in need, they can appear as "generic" angels (wings, robes, halos), or they can appear as your uncle Murray, whom you never met in life but have seen only in family albums, if even there.

The halo that angels traditionally have around their heads in paintings derives originally from the circular scattering of wheat made on a threshing floor. This concreteness is a good thing to keep in mind, because when it comes to envisioning what angels are, the abstract is inevitably the enemy. This is, of course, why Jesus, when explaining truths of incalculable subtlety and difficulty to his puzzled but earnest listeners, always opted for the homeliest, most down-to-earth analogies for what he was talking about.

The word *angel* comes, via old French, from the Greek *angelos*, or messenger. Angels are messengers from God.

Once again in a nutshell, what is their chief message?

That there is another world beyond the filters we have created to block it out—a real world, no less real by a micron for our ignoring this fact. Perhaps we could call angels manifestations, which when we see, feel, and speak to them we categorically cannot doubt, of the world we block out when our helmets are intact. They are the most singularly potent and overwhelming representatives of the world we don't see, the spiritual half of the world that so many today want to pretend doesn't exist at all.

Rilke was not the only great twentieth-century poet to suggest that seeing the world without one's helmet—seeing the spiritual side of the world—is terrifying. "Humankind," the poet T. S. Eliot wrote, "cannot bear very much reality." This sounds abstract, but what Eliot means is that we are such blinkered creatures, by and large, that we have lost our understanding of just how explosively huge the real world—the world that includes the spiritual landscape and not just the physical—really is. Encountering the reality of the spiritual world is not necessarily a soft and cozy experience. In fact, it is generally awful—in the original sense of that word, as "full of awe."

For most of us, the nonspiritual world contains more than enough to frighten us. The daily paper has enough pain in it, if we really appreciated what we were reading about, to send us to the mental hospital. The physical world is terrifying.

But so is the spiritual world. The Bible often describes angels arriving with the words "Fear not." Why? Because they *are* terrifying, just as Rilke suggested. One glimpse of full reality would sweep us away, and angels are ambassadors of full reality.

But, in keeping with their paradoxical nature, they can also protect us from the full blast of that reality. That's why one tradition about guardian angels says that they shield the humans they are assigned to from the divine—from God. Were God's greatness to shine on us fully, we would instantly be destroyed.

Angels represent a reality of which there is no speaking, and they represent it in human form. But by talking about angels— just by giving them a name—we risk losing them. Maybe that's why, early on, the Bible does not have a name for angels at all but calls them simply "men."

One of the singular mysteries of angels is that they show up at times exactly as they are supposed to—with white robes, halos, and wings. To a modern sensibility, this would suggest that they're fantasies. After all, angels, even if they exist, wouldn't really wear white robes, would they? These secondary characteristics were thought up over the course of the centuries, and the characteristics that angels have in our mind today can be—and have been—traced by art historians, cultural historians, and others.

But . . . angels sometimes do show up dressed like that all the same, and try telling someone who has seen one dressed that way that what he saw wasn't real.

That's exactly the essence of the nature of angels—they subvert our expectations at every turn. They demonstrate that reality—*real* reality—is way bigger and stranger than we like to tell ourselves it is. They are always many steps ahead of us.

People who see angels have their ordinary assumptions about what the world is and isn't knocked from them as swiftly and decisively as a gun is knocked from a villain's hand in a movie. That is the message: our assumptions are wrong.

Once knocked away, there is no picking up that old world-view again. There is no talking these people back from what they have seen—no "correcting" them. Even years later, long after the angel has come and gone, there is no getting people back to the old, flat, one-dimensional world in which they lived before. They have stepped out onto the porch of the house of their old understanding, and the door has blown shut behind them.

But angels—the beings that appear in the Old and New Testament—don't simply deliver messages. In and of themselves, they are *the message.*

As mentioned, angels, though by definition messengers, were far from the only messenger beings in the ancient world. India had Hanuman, the monkey god, who served as messenger to the god Rama. Greece had Hermes, who moved quickly and easily between the dark, dank Greek underworld, to the middle world of ordinary mortals, to the blazing, sun-shot overworld of the Olympian gods. Ancient Rome had Mercury—who was basically Hermes tricked out in Roman rather than Greek gear.

An angel is a line drawn straight down into the confusion and darkness of this world from the light-filled world above it.

But angels—the beings that appear in the Old and New Testament—don't simply deliver messages. In and of themselves, they *are* the message.

An angel is a line drawn straight down into the confusion and darkness of this world from the light-filled world above it. In their pure, powerful, unapologetic strangeness, what angels chiefly do in the Bible is *convince*. If we are the type to doubt the existence of God or the world beyond this one, one look at the angel permanently shuts us up.

And Jacob awaked out of his sleep, and he said, Surely the LORD is in this place; and I knew it not.

And he was afraid, and said, How dreadful is this place! this is none other but the house of God, and this is the gate of heaven.

And Jacob rose up early in the morning, and took the stone that he had put for his pillows, and set it up for a

pillar, and poured oil upon the top of it. And he called the
name of that place Bethel: but the name of that city was
called Luz at the first.

GENESIS 28, KING JAMES VERSION

When Jacob comes to the place that he will name Bethel after he has his famous dream of angels ascending and descending a ladder, he says, "How awful is this place." Meaning, how full of awe it is. The world, then and now, is both "awful" in the sense of being a terrible place full of evil and suffering, and "awe-full," in the sense that beyond the fallen world is a larger spiritual one, that places the evil of this world within context. A context which, even now while we are still stuck in this broken world, cures it. The negative aspect of the world is still there, but it cannot overcome us as it did before, because we have seen beyond it.

Both the ladder that Jacob saw and the rock that he used as his pillow are echoes—framed in a manner acceptable to Jewish thought—of an older image: that of the Babylonian ziggurat, or stepped pyramid. In the ages before Judaism arose in the Fertile Crescent, the Jews' predecessors built such pyramid-temples as literal stairways to heaven—places where humans could climb up and interact ceremonially with the gods and goddesses they worshipped.

But for the Jews, of course, building stairways or ladders up to heaven from earth was presumption and could lead only to the kind of outcome that the builders of the Tower of Babel suffered. For humans to make any power-based claims upon the spiritual world means asking to be reduced to confusion, for our understanding of the world is provided by God. If we make a move upon the spiritual, we make a move upon that which has given us our faculty of understanding to begin with, and thus we risk losing that understanding for good.

So it is that the ladder Jacob dreamed of, with angels moving up and down it, was not a ladder built up from earth to heaven, but one let down to earth by God. The suggestion here, of course, is that there is no getting to heaven by human ingenuity, no storming of the walls of the divine by human force. But that doesn't mean heaven is hopelessly sealed off from us. It means that there is indeed commerce between heaven and earth . . . when God wills it.

As we mentioned earlier, the early angels of the Bible lack wings and are often described simply as "men," though typically there is some special atmosphere about them that alerts those who see them that they are not, in fact, ordinary men at all.

Angels often appear to people in trouble. People for whom the world is about to become too much to cope with successfully. However, there is no *making* an angel appear. Angels, by definition, manifest when God wants them to. Like everything else in the spiritual world, they do not show up on command.

Rainer Maria Rilke was acknowledging this fact in his famous long poem *Duino Elegies*, a poem uniquely loaded with angels, when he suggested that it is only when we get to the very edges of life that we can see it clearly. That perilous edge is where the angel dwells; just as we are about to be vanquished by the material world, the supernatural (sometimes at least) steps in and saves us. Rilke was hinting at all of this when he wrote:

For beauty is nothing
but the beginning of terror, which we can just barely endure,
and we stand in awe of it as it coolly disdains
to destroy us. Every angel is terrifying."

It's also probably what the apocryphal gospel of Thomas is talking about when it quotes Jesus as saying: "He who seeks, let him not cease seeking until he finds; and when he finds he will be troubled, and when he is troubled he will be amazed, and he will reign over the All."

Angels change our context. They make us see the whole world instead of the half-world we lived in before.

When an angel-like being appears in the form of someone familiar, such as a grandparent or a recently lost spouse, who—or what—are we to take this being to be? Is it a "ghost" of the individual, an angel in the guise of the family member, or something else? During my years working at *Angels on Earth*, I constantly had to deal with the issue of identity. (In the tremendously common stories of recently lost loved ones who appear in the middle of the night at the foot of the bed of a person suffering from that loss, are we to believe that it really *is* the person who died, or is it an angel representing the person?) Because traditional Christian thought alludes (with greater or lesser degrees of directness, depending on denomination in question) to the concept that the dead are "asleep in God" after death, awaiting the final trumpet before rising in glory, many Christians are uncomfortable with the notion that deceased family members or friends can show up to comfort those they have left behind. The standard solution for this problem at *Angels* was to suggest that, in stories like this,

God presented the individual in question as a kind of facsimile of their friend or relative in order to let them know that this person was okay and safe in heaven.

But is it as simple as that?

As usual, the answer is . . . *probably not*. The fact is that the true fate of the individual following death is a matter of dispute both among Christians and between Christians and other believers in the spiritual world. In the early years of the twentieth century, when a phenomenon called Spiritualism exerted a huge influence on popular thought, the idea grew up that it was possible to be both a Christian and a believer in the possibility that the dead can return, either visibly or audibly, to communicate with the living they had left behind. The intensity of the arguments about this subject that occurred throughout the first decades of the twentieth century might come as a surprise to many today. But in fact, this was an enormous question, both for Christians and non-Christians, and—no surprise—it was never fully resolved.

But it doesn't need to be. Mystics of every age have told us that the spiritual world is so multifaceted, so much subtler and more complex than ordinary physical existence, that it may be that we simply don't have the equipment to answer this question from our present position. As we keep suggesting, the word *angel* doesn't describe a being so much as it describes an action: the communication from the "above" (the heavenly worlds) to the "below" (the flat and ordinary plane of earth), by beings who can appear in a multitude of guises. The Bible describes angels appearing in all manner of ways, from the three strangers who visited Abraham beneath the oaks at Mamre on a sweltering day, to the angel who comforted Hagar in the wilderness, to the being Jacob wrestled with all night, to the dazzling beings sitting at the opening of Christ's tomb on Easter morning, to the wildly alien four-winged circular creatures that manifested to the authors of Ezekiel and Revelation. To say that we have a total grasp of what the biblical writers meant, in our current terms, by these stories is to underestimate the vast variety in which the spiritual worlds, and the beings within them, have appeared to humans.

Like God himself, they are too big for that.

CHAPTER 3

—◦◦—

An Angel Named James Taylor

I was a matron in a boys' school. It was in a country village and when I was off duty in the afternoon there was nothing to do but go for a walk, go into church, or have a quiet time in my room.

One day as I knelt by the fire, my elbows on the chair, I lost the sensation of having a body. I felt a presence across the room and to go nearer I had to pass through a white fire. My spirit did this without feeling anything but happiness and gratitude. The Presence said, "Remember this when you feel you don't belong to you." He looked at me and again told me to remember and I thought, "I could never forget." Then I felt Him leaving, and said, "Won't you come again?" There was a slight pause and He said, "Not like this," and he was gone.

I was back in my body, gazing across the room, and I

felt so full of joy and peace I felt my face must be shining like Moses', but I looked no different.

Years later I had a bad time of anxiety and depression and felt that a high wall separated me from God. I was very unhappy—for a long time. Then I remembered what had happened years before and I think that helped the wall to disappear gradually.

On another occasion I was with a small group and we were finishing a devotional meeting with the Lord's Prayer. Suddenly my spirit was up in the sky and huge clouds were separating to make a wide clear road. There was a noise like thunder and I asked what it meant—and it turned into a loud voice saying, "The Kingdom, the power, and the glory," and I was back in my body to hear people say, "Forever and ever, Amen." I never told anybody about this.

—SEEING THE INVISIBLE

ONCE TYLER HAD broken the ice by asking if anyone else had heard the voice in the car, the four policemen on the Spanish Fork Bridge began discussing the mysterious voice in earnest. Yes, it had been female. Yes, it had been telling them to hurry—that there was not much time. No, at the time of hearing it, no one had doubted that it was a live human being and that it was coming from the inside of the car.

No one, however, seemed ready to take the jump into explaining just how such a thing could be. After all, by the accepted rules that govern the world, what they were discussing—what they had experienced—was impossible. *Group hallucination.*

That was the term Tyler figured someone would give it—some expert on a TV talk show.

But it hadn't been a hallucination. Tyler was sure of it. It had been real. As real as the bite of the frigid water in the river, as real as the metal of the wrecked car that had cut into him, and as real as the slow throb at the back of his head where he'd banged it during the rescue.

Tyler decided right then and there that he wasn't going to be quiet about what had happened. If someone asked, he'd tell the truth. After all, when was it ever wrong for a cop to tell the truth?

Within hours, the story of the miracle baby who'd survived a night in an upside-down car with only her dead mother for company was all over the news. First the local stations picked it up, then the nationals, and the following night Tyler found himself in the novel situation of sitting with Warner and two of the firemen who'd been present at the rescue, telling CNN's Anderson Cooper about the event.

The story, it turned out, had all the elements that make for broad public interest. There was tragedy, in the form of Jennifer's death. There was hope, in the form of Lily's all-but-inexplicable survival. There was heroism, in the form of Tyler and the other officers, firemen, and EMT workers who had braved the water to get Lily out. And there was, over and above that, the voice: the mysterious words urging the four officers on—telling them to hurry up, because there wasn't much time. That voice, in turn, led to what seemed to be the most powerful element of all: the idea that somehow, through those long, dark hours of stark, horrific solitude, someone had been "with" Lily.

Who is with us? Are we alone, or are we not alone? More than all the other spark plugs for media attention, that was the key reason Jenny's death and Lily's survival became not just local or national news, but a world story. It was a question that resonated.

And pretty much overnight, Officer Tyler Beddoes found himself, to his surprise and perplexity, the poster boy for it. Six-foot-two, classically handsome but with a boyish, innocent look and curiously round head that made him look a little like a *Peanuts* character grown up, Tyler played well on camera. Down at the precinct his supervisor, dealing with the increasing flood of calls about the story, told Tyler, "You're comfortable with this thing and you sound good. From now on I'm sending you out whenever I get a request for an interview."

This was fine with Tyler. After ten years on the force he knew well enough what to say to reporters. He knew better than to tart the story up, to tell anything other than what he had experienced. The facts were always enough.

Plus, as a police officer, he was well aware of the fact that in the America of spring 2015, an inspiring story might be a nice change of pace for people. It seemed as if everywhere you looked, things were going badly, and going fast from bad to worse. The economy was still a wreck. Jobs were still down, and had been down for so long that it was starting to get hard to remember a time when they weren't. All through the West, the unprecedented heat waves of the last few summers had farmers dreading what was to come this time around. The world, always going to hell in a handbasket, was showing signs that it was now doing so in a new, different, larger kind of way. There were weeks when it seemed as if nothing, absolutely nothing, positive was happening anywhere. If the mysterious survival of a baby in a creek bed would give people a little hope, Tyler was happy to step up and be the mouthpiece for it.

The drawbacks of modern American instant celebrity, however, soon made themselves apparent. "I can't look at those tapes," Tyler told me about the recordings that his mom, Pam, had made. "All those clips of me talking on the TV shows— I'm too afraid I'll look like an idiot. I think it might also look like I'm trying to grab all this attention for myself for what happened. I'm not, though. The other guys were fine with me being the one to tell the story. Harward, he said no way to the media stuff from the start. He's real private, and the last thing he wanted was his face on TV stations all over the world. DeWitt and Warner were the same way. They were like, 'You want to talk to all those cameras, go ahead.' So I just ended up being the one telling the story of what happened again and again. It was crazy. But I don't regret it, at least not yet. I mean, what I say happened really *did* happen. We heard that voice. It just seemed to me like it was a message the world should know about. It means something. Especially when the rest of the story, the story of the mom, was so sad. I was helping make other people feel better. And I wasn't lying to do it. I was telling the God's-honest truth about something just crazy that happened, and that I was there for, and that three other guys who are rock solid and reliable were there for, too. So even though it was weird and right away I started getting these phone calls about movies and God knows what and I thought, 'What am I getting into here?'— even so, at bottom I was making people feel better. And there just didn't seem to me to be anything wrong with that."

Making people feel better—or perhaps more simply, helping them—had been an aspiration of Tyler's for as long as he or anyone who knows him can remember. Tyler and his brother, Zack, four years older than he, grew up in Benjamin, a small suburb of Spanish Fork, in a house next to his maternal grandparents, Anna and Donald. Behind the two rambler-style houses there were alfalfa fields where Tyler's grandparents' sheep and cows and goats grazed. There was a good amount of space between houses in the neighborhood, but not so much that Tyler and his brother felt isolated. Many of those houses had kids, and Tyler enjoyed the kind of three-dimensional, nondigital childhood that is becoming so rare in America these days. He had no PlayStation, iPhones were years away, and his favorite game was cops and robbers with the other neighborhood kids. Tyler always played the cop.

Like most of the population of Spanish Fork, Tyler's grandparents were Mormon. They went to the regular Sunday meetings but never tried to cram the faith down Tyler's throat. Tyler's granddad had done graduate work at UCLA in forest ecology, and the general attitude Tyler absorbed from his parents and grandparents was that the world is a good place and that it is everyone's job to lead a good, responsible life, taking advantage of what God has provided but respecting it, too, and helping others do so as well.

The result was an environment in which God hovered, for Tyler, somewhere in the background, with not too many tangible attributes other than the obvious ones a kid would imagine. He was good, he loved his creation, and he wanted people to do and live right. Life was worth living, and other lives deserved honoring and protecting. As for the small points, the doctrinaire arguments about what made one church different from an-other, Tyler didn't spend too much time worrying about all that. Who needed all that fine print? The world was a good place, people were generally good, too, and the evidence for that was all around. Maybe that was all you were going to know about how things worked on earth, but maybe that was all you really needed to know.

Tyler seemed to have absorbed a good bit of this basic philosophy from his dad. Tyler's mom and dad were both raised Mormon, but his mom was much more active in the church than his dad was. "He was supportive of the faith, no question," said Tyler. "But he had a problem with the whole middleman thing. Did God really need some complicated set of self-appointed experts telling people what he was like and how he wanted humans to behave? My dad was always at my basketball games and my football games. He was the best dad you could ask for. Some folks—the real down-the-line LDS (Latter-Day Saints) people—said he wasn't living right, that they didn't hardly ever see him in church, you know, all that stuff. Dad knew they said as much, but that was okay. He knew what he knew; he had no doubt that there was a God up there, and he felt like if he wasn't perfect in God's eyes, he probably wasn't alone in that. After all, if going to church made you a good person and not going made you a bad one, then 'good' and 'bad' must have had different meanings than he thought they did. I know how he feels. You know—some people are all hugs and kisses on Sunday and jerks the other six days of the week. That's not the way my dad was when I was growing up, and I think that lesson meant a lot to me."

One thing that struck me about Tyler right away was his

combination of forthrightness and courtesy—the way his native honesty was matched by a deep concern that he not wound anyone with his words. Many people are guarded when they speak to writers—as well they should be. But Tyler wasn't guarded during our initial talks so much as careful. He was not—as he might have put it when in a particularly forthright mood—looking to cover his own rear end. However, he *was* always anxious that something might slip out that would end up hurting someone's feelings. And that sentiment seemed to extend to the Mormon church itself, which Tyler treated as a beloved if sometimes irascible uncle. It was there, it had always been there, he liked it fine, and if he didn't spend as much time with it as some others did, well, that was just how it was.

If the world wasn't a completely perfect place, Tyler got his first really solid taste of this fact in a sad but classic way. He got his first dog, a spaniel named Lucky, when he was nine.

"We'd had other dogs, but Lucky was specifically my dog," Tyler told me. "I took care of him, fed him; he was my responsibility. We were pretty much inseparable. We lived on a dead-end lane. One guy, a neighbor, always drove like a bat out of hell. Mom and Dad would get frustrated. You know, 'That so-and-so needs to slow down, there's kids playing on this street.'"

One day Lucky happened to be in the road when the neighbor sped by, and he got hit. Tyler saw the whole thing. He ran down and held his dog, still panting but fatally injured, and watched, helpless, as he died in his arms. The guy got out of his car. "Sorry, kid," he said. "I'll buy you a new one."

"My mom was there," Tyler said. "She was bawling. Not so much because of Lucky but because she could see what witnessing that had done to me. I cussed that guy out like crazy, called him a bastard and a murderer. You know, something like that, when you're a kid, can really shake your picture of things. At least that's what it did with me."

Tyler's parents tried to comfort him in the usual way parents do in such circumstances. "They were like, 'When you die you go to a better place. . . ' Stuff like that. But I wasn't so sure I believed it. I wanted to believe it, but I just wasn't so sure I did anymore. I mean, here I named my dog Lucky, and just by doing that I figured I'd made sure he was going to be a lucky dog. I learned a lesson about the difference between words and reality that day."

On TV, the 1990s and early 2000s were the time of the forensic cop, and Tyler got hooked on shows like *CSI* and *Forensic Files*. He loved watching the forces of good team up with science to solve the most seemingly unsolvable crimes. He loved the way the smallest, most ridiculously easy-to-overlook detail could lead investigators to criminals who'd thought they'd gotten away with (usually) murder. A single hair, a piece of filament from the back of a van, or some other minute thing would turn out to be a finger pointing across hundreds of miles, and maybe years, directly at the bad guy. Those shows were Tyler's first hint that if the world didn't make total sense, then this wasn't something people just needed to stand by and watch. Praying to God might work for some, but Tyler gravitated more to the cops, detectives, and forensic specialists on these shows: people who saw that the world was often a pretty bad place, and instead of asking God how come he'd made it that way, stepped in to do something about it.

For Tyler, "good" and "bad" were not the only polarities of which the world was made. Those forensics shows often carried with them a hint of mystery—a mystery that lingered even after the crime had been solved and the malefactor had been caught and sent off to jail or the electric chair. The world didn't hold just good and bad. It held the ordinary and the mysterious, that sense that there was always something left unsolved even after all the questions had been answered. . . . If Tyler didn't possess much of a religious streak, he did possess a bit of a philosophical one, and those crime shows satisfied that side of him, too. Even when you got to the bottom of things, it seemed, there was usually still something left. Why was the world—*all* the world, the way it was? Even when an episode of *CSI* or *Forensic Files* tied up the specific case in question, those other, larger questions still remained.

Tyler's mom had a brother named Eddie. "He was as big as me," Tyler told me. "Your typical all-American kid, I guess you could say. He was real athletic. He went to play college baseball at Dixie State U in St. George, Utah, on a scholarship. Things were looking real good for him. So one day he notices this bump on his leg. Just this little thing, something you'd hardly even give any thought to. Except that it wouldn't go away. It turns out that it's bone cancer. Nineteen years old, and he's got cancer. It hit my grandparents like a ton of bricks. In a couple of months he went from being the healthiest-looking guy you've ever seen to a ghost. The doctors didn't give him a long time to live, so he came home to die. Grandma shared the story of his last day with me. He was on a lot of painkillers, and he was lying in the living room, all hooked up to stuff. By that point the cancer had metastasized and it had destroyed his corneas. So on top of everything else, he was totally blind. But on that day, he suddenly looked up to the corner of the room and said, 'Hey, Mom, he's here to get me. Can I go?'

"Grandma asked him, 'Who's here, dear?'

"'James Taylor,' my uncle Eddie said."

"James Taylor?" I asked just to make sure I'd heard correctly.

"Yup," Tyler said. "Eddie said, 'James Taylor is here to get me.' That didn't make a whole lot of sense to Grandma either, but she said, 'Honey, if that's what you want to do, you can go.' And she kissed his forehead. And just like that, he went."

CHAPTER 4

―――――∽⚬∽―――――

Describing the Indescribable

*And every one had four faces, and every one had four wings.
And their feet were straight feet; and the sole of their feet
was like the sole of a calf's foot: and they sparkled like the
colour of burnished brass. And they had the hands of a man
under their wings on their four sides; and they four had their
faces and their wings. Their wings were joined one to another; they turned not when they went; they went every one
straight forward. As for the likeness of their faces, they four
had the face of a man, and the face of a lion, on the right
side: and they four had the face of an ox on the left side; they
four also had the face of an eagle. Thus were their faces: and
their wings were stretched upward; two wings of every one
were joined one to another, and two covered their bodies.
And they went every one straight forward: whither the spirit
was to go, they went; and they turned not when they went.
As for the likeness of the living creatures, their appearance
was like burning coals of fire, and like the appearance of
lamps: it went up and down among the living creatures; and
the fire was bright, and out of the fire went forth lightning.*

And the living creatures ran and returned as the appearance
of a flash of lightning. Now as I beheld the living creatures,
behold one wheel upon the earth by the living creatures,
with his four faces. The appearance of the wheels and their
work was like unto the colour of a beryl: and they four had
one likeness: and their appearance and their work was as
it were a wheel in the middle of a wheel. When they went,
they went upon their four sides: and they turned not when
they went.

—EZEKIEL 1, KING JAMES VERSION

W HEN WE LOOK up into the sky, we do not see the same thing
that a peasant from the Middle Ages would have seen. For him
or her, the fixed stars and the wandering stars, in their related
yet subtly different shifts of position through the seasons, suggested a series of heavenly bands or levels, each watched over by
a different angelic intelligence. In this view, which a member of
that society didn't experience abstractly but as vividly as he or
she experienced the people and objects of earth, each set of stars
represented an ever-subtler rung on the staircase of angelic levels: levels that led, ultimately, to the empyrean—the highest part
of heaven, where God dwelt in his infinite majesty.

The angels that dwelt in these different levels were beings
who, while exhibiting a different kind of intelligence from
that of humans, were not cut off from human intelligence and
human reality. They were creatures of the same cosmos and creations of the same God, so no matter if it might be difficult to
understand or even picture them, the cosmic family connection

we humans shared with them prevented them from ever becoming "alien" in any modern sense of the term. The world, after all, might have been fallen, and satanic evil and human sin might have been to blame for that fall, but it was still one world. And the Fall, terrible as it was, took place within a larger narrative of revolt and ultimate redemption: a drama in which the angels, both the good and (of course) the bad ones had key roles to play. Because of all these facts, the lowest peasant, gazing at the night sky, sensed in her bones her profound connection and communion with those worlds above.

Imagining what it might have been like to live in such a densely populated universe of matter and spirit is difficult from our perspective, where for many people the night sky appears as vast and beautiful, but essentially chaotic and empty—a place of extreme temperatures and impossible distances, completely bereft of human or spiritual meaning.

The need to map out the cosmos in terms of the kinds of angels that inhabited it arose early on. The first detailed description of angelic hierarchies came from a fifth-century AD writer named Dionysius the Areopagite—or, as he is more commonly known, Pseudo-Dionysius. The "pseudo" comes from the fact that Dionysius, while framing himself as a certain Dionysius who was a contemporary of Saint Paul's, in fact wrote his tract on the celestial hierarchies and his other celebrated works some five centuries after Paul's time. The practice of taking the name of an illustrious predecessor was common in the ancient world, and the fact that Pseudo-Dionysius was not the Dionysius he claimed to be shouldn't detract from his writings, which have a surprising life and resonance even for a modern reader.

Whether one is of a faith that believes in angelic hierarchies or not, the most important thing to take away from Pseudo-Dionysius's vision of the hierarchies is the idea—central to Catholic thinkers such as Saint Thomas Aquinas as well—that angelic intelligence is ordered and alive from top to bottom. Far from the marvelous but ultimately meaningless swirl of matter and energy that materialism sees when it looks at the night sky, the old Dionysian/Thomist universe is a genuinely living thing. According to the Dionysian system, the guardian angels are at the bottom of the angelic ladder, which makes sense when we consider that they are the ones entrusted with helping us on our way through life. Above these are a series of higher levels of angels, extremely difficult for us to envisage, which exercise a broader and more distanced influence on worldly doings: the powers and principalities are said to govern entire countries, while the levels above them are ceaselessly worshipping God.

> *The world is, quite simply, more complicated than many of us take it to be, and this is especially the case when we come to the mysteries of perception: of what is there and what is not there.*

The highest orders—the cherubim and seraphim—are so impossibly distanced from us that it is not hard to believe that many of the UFO encounters reported in recent decades might have to do with them. This does not mean that the floating disks so many people have reported in the twentieth and twenty-first centuries are literally these angelic beings. Things angelic are never as simple as that. But the overlaps between the ways UFOs look to the modern people who have seen them and the way the higher, stranger angels looked to the ancient people who saw them are (as many have pointed out) suggestive. Suggestive of what? That UFOs are "really" angels? That angels are "really" UFOs? Both . . . and neither. As usual in this area, those in search of absolutely solid, two-plus-two-equals-four answers are out of luck. The world is, quite simply, more complicated than many of us take it to be, and this is especially the case when we come to the mysteries of perception: of what is there and what is not there.

Cherubim, the Old Testament relates, were set up at the entrance of Eden to bar Adam and Eve from attempting to reenter it. They also appear on the ark of the covenant in Exodus and elsewhere. These beings, from which the word *cherub* developed, were far from the cute and cuddly floating babies we tend to associate with the name. Originally they were large, four-legged beings whose appearance echoed the massive and similarly named winged gods that appeared in cities of the ancient Near East long before the arrival of the Hebrews.

Envisioning Ezekiel's description of the cherubim is difficult, yet these beings have a clear enough message for us: in their roundness they are whole beings. Second, they are covered with eyes. This, at first pass, sounds either bizarre or simply grotesque. These beings initially seem more like something from a fifties monster movie than from heaven. But the rhetorical style of the prophets is not always easy for a modern reader to find his or her way into, just as with the fantastically image-rich language of John of Patmos in Revelation. In trying to come to terms with the angelic beings that Ezekiel and John of Patmos describe, we have to take the key features they have and override our initial desire simply to picture an earthly being with these qualities. What we have to do instead is take the three chief features that the higher angelic beings are described as having—roundness, wings, and eyes—and imagine what a creature that is more than we can physically imagine might be like if it were characterized above all by these features. What we get if we do this is a being that can see everywhere (omniscience), move everywhere (omnipotence), and which is completely whole. Nothing is hidden from it, nothing is unreachable to it, and (spiritually speaking) it lacks for nothing. That is the truth hiding behind the more bizarre descriptions of angelic beings in the Bible that have puzzled so many readers.

The keynote of creation is variety.

The keynote of creation is variety. One of the most beautiful books I ever came across (I stumbled on it in a library) was an enormous volume filled with plates of hundreds of intricately rendered paintings. The subject of the paintings, and of the book, was the different varieties of crabs found in a single bay in Japan.

If we look around and take into consideration the vast number of species in the material world, and the lines of similarity (and dissimilarity) among them, the notion that the spiritual worlds contain such a variety becomes quite easy to believe.

By suggesting that the chain of creation does not stop at the visible world but continues beyond it, we are making an argument much stressed by Saint Thomas Aquinas—an individual who wrote a great deal on angels (and devils). It's an argument that makes sense—not just in Aquinas's time, but ours. To grasp it requires only that we grant that the hierarchy of God's creation might not stop precisely at the spot where the recording instruments for reality currently at our disposal do. The deeps of the sea were long thought by science to be completely empty—until we developed the technology to get down there and see for ourselves. Surprise of surprises, they were teeming with life, and a lot of the creatures discovered there were so bizarre that it was at first hard for the initial explorers of those depths to believe what they were seeing.

For our purposes, the angelic beings most of interest are those closest to us: the guardian angels who have been tasked with looking out for us while we writhe and struggle through the confusions of material existence. This is the level whose "job" is to watch us closely as we go through the rough and bumpy burlesque of our lives, attempting to give advice when it seems most possible that this advice will be taken seriously.

Not all faith traditions believe in guardian angels—Catholics usually do; most Evangelicals do not. But no matter what one's position, it is an interesting exercise to understand how someone who *does* believe in these beings experiences them, to understand what a living relationship with the angelic hierarchies—particularly the guardian angels that are "closest" to us, spiritually speaking—is like.

If you are a pet owner, you will have an easier time conceiving what this relationship might look like. You love your dog. Your dog loves you. That is clear. And yet, you are beings that possess entirely different styles of intelligence. Your dog understands some things, yet is hopelessly and bewilderingly unable to understand others. You are, cognitively speaking, superior to your dog. Does that mean you are better than your dog? Not in the least. You are simply plugged into a different landscape of understanding. You are at home with abstractions. Your dog is not. On the other hand, you walk into a forest with little awareness of the life it contains. Your dog, meanwhile, steps into the woods the way you surf the Internet. Information, via the dog's sharpened senses, comes in from every direction, and the dog instantly and easily knows how to read it. So much so, in fact, that he can get impatient with you when you (inexplicably to him) fail to pick up on some crucial piece of information, like the fact that a mere ten paces off the trail you are on, a three-days-dead squirrel cries out for closer inspection. How dumb can one be?

You and your dog get along great. You understand and respect each other, in the way that fellow beings should. All the same, you are different. As a human, you have been gifted not just with consciousness, as your dog has, but with self-consciousness. That means that you not only know about things, but *you know that you know* about things. You are one step further up the ladder of existence than your dog is.

Does that mean that you can't genuinely connect with your dog, that you can't keenly love it and suffer terribly when it dies? Absolutely not. You and your dog, representatives of different bands on the ladder of being, are capable of being true friends despite all the vast differences of perception and understanding that divide you.

I don't know what guardian angels look like. (If you are open to getting an opinion on the matter, consult the works of the modern Irish mystic Lorna Byrne, who has seen angels since childhood and describes them in overwhelming detail in several books.) But I can, to a degree and thanks to the relationships with animals that I've enjoyed over the course of my life, extrapolate what my relationship to an angel might be like.

My guardian angel sees me—all of me. While I drift in and out of connection with my real self, sometimes floating perilously far away from it and sometimes coming wonderfully close, my guardian angel does not have to suffer theses vagaries of distance. He (or she, or it; opinions differ) is always in touch with the real me, even if I am not. If there is one chief duty of the guardian angel, it is to keep us in contact with the being we are at our truest and deepest—to not let the distractions and attractions of the world so pull us off our center that we lose touch with who we truly are. I suspect that, if guardian angels *do* exist, they must suffer quite a bit of pain as they watch what their individual charges do down here on earth and how often they fall into foolishness and falsity.

Physicality is, if nothing else, a fiendishly well-designed place for losing track of one's true identity. But in the end, there is no escaping that identity, no escaping who we truly are or at least were meant to be. According to an ancient Persian tradition, we will, at death, meet our angel—that being in the spiritual world that has been monitoring our odyssey in the physical world, year by year and moment by moment. If our behavior has been bad—

if we, through our actions in life, betrayed the ideal that was set up for us before we were born—then the face of our angel will be terrifying. It will manifest, in visual form, the ugliness of what our straying from the true path looks like. (High school readers of Oscar Wilde's *The Picture of Dorian Gray* will recognize what's going on here.)

> *Goodness, as it turns out, is not to be trifled with. It is not to be bullied. It is not to be compromised. Nothing can touch it.*

But if we have lived a life in sync with our angel (which, I'll stress again, does not mean a life of simply following the rules, of simply doing what others tell us, but of following our heart), then the being we meet at death will not be horrible, but beautiful beyond imagining. Goodness, love—these are real things, not abstractions. They are as real as kerosene, as real as explosions that level buildings. Goodness, as it turns out, is not to be trifled with. It is not to be bullied. It is not to be compromised. Nothing can touch it. And it seems that, though the individuals involved in angelic encounters may not always express it this way, angels' behavior delivers the same essential message. In this world where everything seems corruptible, there is a level of being that is acutely aware of the difficulties of this world but not (even remotely) touched by it. Angels comfort, angels heal, angels (sometimes) terrify. But most important, they manifest, and in that manifestation lies their singular gift to humankind.

It's an odd fact, but a fact all the same, that the single most inexplicable example of guardian angels entering into the human world happened just two hundred miles northeast of Spanish Fork as the crow flies. Not too far from the Utah-Wyoming border, there lies a little town called Cokeville. Some thirty years ago, the citizens of Cokeville were witness to the single largest act of domestic terrorism at that point in American history. On a blustery spring day in May of 1986, a man named David Young arrived at the Cokeville Elementary School in a large van with the windows painted over so that no one could see its contents. With him were his teenage daughter Princess; his wife, Doris; and a homemade bomb designed to kill every child in the school.

> *"I don't know how the wires were cut. My only official conclusion is that I can't begin to explain it."*
> —BOMB EXPERT RICHARD HASKELL ON THE
> CUT WIRES TO THE BLASTING CAPS IN THE
> COKEVILLE BOMB

Cokeville was and is a town much like Spanish Fork. Like Spanish Fork it was born with the Mormon migration in the mid- and late 1800s. Like Spanish Fork it is still largely Mormon. And like Spanish Fork it is an example of what an American town can be at its best: a place where different people with different ideas about politics, religion, and whatever else live in a spirit of mutual respect and togetherness.

Cokeville also has an excellent school system, something David

Young knew well, because several years before the day that he pulled up at Cokeville Elementary in his van, he had spent a brief time as Cokeville's sheriff. Young had not lasted long in the position because, as one member of the Cokeville Police Force said, he was "more interested in being Wyatt Earp than a good cop."

The bomb that Young brought to Cokeville Elementary that day didn't look like much to an untrained eye. Housed in a shopping cart procured from a local supermarket, it was composed of a gallon jug of gasoline, a large battery, and a series of "blasting caps"—containers with a highly volatile mix of gunpowder, powdered aluminum, and powdered chromium. The principle of the bomb was that an initial explosion would cause the containers of powdered metal to blow up and disperse through the air. A second explosion would then ignite those particles, in effect creating a solid block of pure fire. Among bomb experts, it was known as a "dead man's bomb," for the simple reason that it was extremely effective at killing large amounts of people.

Young, with his wife and daughter behind him, rolled the shopping cart up to the receptionist, who gave him a friendly hello and asked how she could be of help. Young announced that he was taking over the school and demanding a ransom of two million dollars for every child in it. Young gathered all the students and teachers into a single classroom and outlined his intentions to children and adults alike. Pointing to two safety pins connecting a bracelet on his wrist to the bomb by way of a long shoelace, Young explained that should anyone do anything he didn't like, he would give his wrist the mildest of jerks, the safety pins would come apart, and the bomb would ignite, killing Young and everyone else in the room, and flattening the entire school as well.

That Young meant business—and was clearly deranged—
became fully apparent to the teachers when he had Doris pass out
mimeographed pages laying out his personal philosophy. (Right
after entering the school, Princess had lost her nerve and fled,
so the task of assisting Young fell entirely on his wife.) Young's
situation was this: Tired (as he saw it) of being smarter than everyone else yet having to suffer the indignities of employment
by individuals inferior to him, he had plunged into a solitary
study of the nature of the world. This study had eventually led
him to develop a philosophy of his own. In this philosophy, no
God existed, but reincarnation did. The children of Cokeville
Elementary were extremely fortunate, for David was planning
on taking all of them with him to die and be reincarnated on a
planet where he would become their own private god, instruct-
ing them in the ways of the universe and developing a whole
new civilization of truly educated beings.

Cokeville was the perfect town for Young to use to launch his
plan for two reasons: its children were very well educated and
hence would make great pupils for him in the world to come,
and the town itself would be very easy to manipulate. Why?
Because in the course of his time there he had come to appreciate what a tight-knit community it was. Everyone in Cokeville,
Young knew, cared for everyone else. And this was especially
the case when it came to their children. By kidnapping all those
children at once, Young thought he would instantly make the
town putty in his hands.

Young was, to say the least, a seriously unbalanced individual, but he was so in a way that grimly prefigured the behavior of the lone-wolf terrorists who have created so many ugly

headlines in America in recent years. In a world without true community, the evidence would suggest, David Youngs multiply like rabbits. When David Young took over Cokeville Elementary with his homemade bomb and homemade philosophy, however, the occurrence raised eyebrows across the country and beyond much more than it would today. That is because Young was, in terms of his derangement, way ahead of his time, and what he attempted at Cokeville became one of the first examples of what can happen when people abandon not just civic but spiritual community and drift off into themselves.

In charge of communicating between Young and the outside world was the school's principal, Max Excell. At one point, Hartt and Judene Wixom write in their excellent book on the event, *When Angels Intervene to Save the Children*, "Excell thought the man was calm enough to risk a question. 'Why this school?' he asked, keeping his voice very low. 'Why here?' "

To Excell's surprise, Young answered.

"Because this is a family town," Young told Excell, "where people love their children, and they'll do anything to get them back."

As the afternoon dragged on, the teachers did everything they could to keep the kids calm, encouraging them to play games and talk quietly among themselves. Sitting by his deadly contraption, Young was quiet most of the time, but as the minutes ticked by he seemed to grow more sullen. It fell to Doris to communicate Young's wishes to the kids and the adults. Some of the kids later recalled that she had seemed like a "nice lady," while others had felt she was as "bad" as the man with the beard in the center of the room.

At 2:00 p.m., the teachers started to notice that in addition to being hot and stuffy, the classroom was filling up with a sweet, queasy, familiar smell. Gasoline was leaking from a small crack in the gallon jug that Young had procured for his bomb that morning. Before too long the children began to feel sick, and some started throwing up. A teacher dared asking Young to open the windows, and he agreed.

At 3:45, Young decided he needed to go to the bathroom. The room watched petrified as Young removed the shoelace trigger from his own wrist and put it on Doris's.

Leaving Doris, Young headed for the bathroom. The Wixoms continue:

> *Once David was out of sight, the children relaxed. But with the removal of the tension he generated, they immediately became more restless and noisy as well. "Children!" said Jean Mitchell, "we need 'Quiet Time.'" In the mounting hubbub, she was beginning to feel ill. David had not reappeared and Jean did not want him suddenly walking out into even the semblance of disorder and confusion. Raising her hand to her head, she admitted to Doris, "I've got a headache."*

Doris knew just how she felt. She'd had the same horrible headache from the gas fumes for some time. She reached her hand to her own forehead in sympathy. And as her hand went up, it yanked the string, just ever so slightly, and the two clips disengaged. The bomb went off.

Pandemonium is an interesting word. It was first coined by

John Milton when he wanted a name for the stronghold of fallen angels who sought to rise and enter Eden to corrupt Adam and Eve in *Paradise Lost*. In its more modern meaning, it describes exactly what followed after the bomb went off. Smoke and flames filled the room. Screaming children and teachers struggling to get them to the windows and out to safety moved around in a thick cloud of smoke that obscured practically everything.

Emerging from the bathroom, Young saw one of the male teachers running for the exit doors and shot him in the back. The bullet missed his heart by an inch, leaving him seriously but not critically wounded. He kept running, escaped the school, and lived.

The next person Young saw was his wife, Doris, who had received the brunt of the bomb's force and was running out of the classroom, covered in flames. Young dropped to one knee and expertly placed one shot through her head (out of anger or out of compassion for her state, no one knows). Next he saw one of the female teachers, Eva Clark, who was leading a troop of her students to the exit doors as well. Clark and Young looked at each other, and Clark was sure she was dead. But Young didn't shoot. Instead he turned, went back to the bathroom, sat down on the tiny toilet he had just left, put his favorite, personally engraved pistol under his chin, and fired.

Choking on the black smoke and not knowing if Young was still alive and a threat, police and rescue personnel swarmed into the building. Hysterical parents, having waited out the long afternoon, struggled to get in as well. How many children had been killed? How many teachers?

As the smoke cleared and the rescuers continued picking

among the wreckage, the incredible truth emerged. Only two people had died in the explosion: David Young and his wife, Doris. Some of the kids and teachers had been burned, a few severely, and some severely enough that they would have to endure weeks or months of painful recovery. But no one else died.

Given the power of the bomb and Young's ingenuity in building it, how could this have happened?

The remains of the bomb were examined by a local explosives expert named Richard Haskell. Taking the device apart, he discovered something remarkable. Two of the wires connecting the battery to the blasting caps had been clipped, preventing the juice from getting to them when Doris tripped the bomb. Because of this, the power of the bomb had been radically diminished. But why were the wires clipped? No one had had access to the bomb other than David, and he certainly was not the one to have clipped them. The fact that the wires were clipped simply made no sense. Yet all the same, there it was.

Further strange discoveries followed. It turned out that the crack in the one-gallon plastic jug that contained the gas for the bomb had caused gas to drip down onto the blasting caps, turning the powder within them into a paste that was far less deadly when the bomb finally went off than it would have been had the powder stayed dry. So not only did some of the blasting caps not explode, but those that did, exploded with only a fraction of the force they would have, had the gas not leaked onto them.

There was something stranger still. Instead of blowing straight out, as a dead man's bomb normally would have, the bomb blew *up*, so that the main force of the flames struck the ceiling of the classroom, the soft tiles of which absorbed most of its heat and power. That portion of the force and fire the ceiling didn't absorb flared out and down the walls: walls that very few of the kids and teachers in the room were standing near. It blew so that the one person to receive its brunt was the person who set it off—David's wife, Doris.

Why had the force of the bomb traveled up instead of out? The Wixoms narrate how what appeared to be the only possible answer came to light.

> Seven-year-old Katie Walker told her fourteen-year-old brother, Shane, the first family member she saw after running from the explosion, "They saved us. I said a prayer, and they saved us!"
>
> "Who saved you?" Shane asked.
>
> "The angels," she replied.
>
> Katie saw her mother, Glenna Walker, a few minutes later. "Mommy," Katie repeated, "the angels saved us!"
>
> Glenna patted her daughter on the head. "Yes, we all have much to be grateful for, dear," she said, holding her close.
>
> Glenna did not realize that her daughter wanted to be taken literally. Even though Katie's sister Rachel was being treated for burns at the hospital, Rachel and Katie and Travis had all come through their ordeal alive and Glenna hoped they would soon no longer need to talk about the takeover. The children, however, wanted to talk about it.
>
> Dr. Vern Cox was one of the psychologists brought in to help the town work through the fears and feelings generated by David Young's attack. Along with other families in

Cokeville, Kevin and Glenna joined the group and individual discussions intended to provide this help. At one of these meetings, Katie and Rachel told Dr. Cox that they had tried to talk with their parents about the angels who had saved them. Their brother Travis also had something very serious on his mind. Dr. Cox told their parents what the children had been telling him.

"Why haven't they been telling us, their own parents?" Glenna wanted to know.

"Have you been listening to them?" he asked her. "Really listening?"

Glenna realized that perhaps they hadn't. She and Kevin arranged a time when the whole family could talk.

"They were standing there above us," Katie began. "There was a mother and a father and a lady holding a tiny baby, and a little girl with long hair. There was a family of people. The woman told us the bomb was going off soon, and to listen to our brother. He was going to come over and tell us what to do."

"She said to be sure we did what he told us," Rachel added.

"They were all dressed in white, bright like a light bulb but brighter around the face," Katie told her mother.

"The girl had a long dress," Rachel nodded, "which covered her feet, and she had light brown hair."

The two girls spoke quietly but firmly about people who had certainly not been among the hostages. There was no apology or self-consciousness—the people they described seemed as real to them as their own parents, who were listening, attentively now. Rachel remembered something else—that the figures dressed in white standing above them had moved around to another part of the room just before the bomb went off.

Other children saw nothing, but heard distinct directions. "I didn't see anything—nothing!" said one. "I just heard a voice. It told me to find my little sisters and take them over by the window and keep them there. I did what I was told."

Child after child told his or her story of what had happened just before the explosion: of beings clothed in white that had descended through the ceiling, given the children specific instructions about where to go, and formed a ring around the bomb, a ring that appears to be the only explicable reason that the blast, diminished as it was, went up toward the ceiling, then down the walls, rather than out, where it would have done much more harm.

Some thirty years after Cokeville, the singular mystery of the event stands as strong as ever. No one has explained it, and no one has robbed it of its terror or magic. It is a story of the world as it really is: a world of evil and good, of things visible and invisible. If it is not proof of angels, it is certainly proof that the world is more than we tend to think it is.

CHAPTER 5

The Academy

After the sudden death of a four-and-a-half-year-old son, I found no comfort in anything or anyone; the church seemed powerless to help me, as did the medical profession. I could not go out of the flat I was living in at that time and, although I tried very hard, I could see nothing but blackness and an intense longing to die. One morning I was dusting, tidying, the usual household chores, when I smelled the most wonderful garden flowers. It is difficult to describe the smell I mean—rather like a garden after rain. Being of a somewhat practical mind in such things, I looked around for the source of the smell. There were no flowers in the flat, certainly none outside, no perfumed polishes or toilet things in use. Then I sat down and for the first time since my son died I felt peaceful inside. I believe this was God's comfort; my son felt very near and I no longer felt alone.

All I can tell you now is that I have no fear of what we call death. To me it will be shedding the material life for a spiritual life and although I have had no great revelations, I shall try to live according to His divine plan and be ready to leave when He is ready for me.

—SEEING THE INVISIBLE

TYLER'S BROTHER, ZACK, four years older, was different from Tyler in his approach to life—in particular, the church. He was there every Sunday, and he took to the Mormon lifestyle like a fish to water.

"He absolutely believed," Tyler told me. "And he does now, too. I think the faith has been really good for him. We slept in the same room growing up. Sunday mornings, he'd shout over to me that it was time to get up for church. Usually, I'd give him an 'I ain't going,' and turn over and go back to sleep. But he didn't get all high-and-mighty about it. Nobody in my family did. I think that might be why I still feel like I have a good relationship with my faith even if I'm not in it up to my chin like my brother. If I'd been pushed to get up and drag myself off every Sunday, I think I might just hate it now. I got a couple of friends who are exactly that way for exactly that reason."

One thing Tyler wasn't lukewarm about was what he wanted to do in life. He was going to be a cop. The decision might have been made when he was just a kid in front of the TV, but it didn't go away as he got older. As soon as he was twenty, he was going to join the local academy.

The decision was a hard one for Tyler's mom, Pam, when she realized her son was really serious—that it was going to happen.

"I used to lie awake at night," she told me, "so torn up about it. I just couldn't imagine my boy going off to a job every day where . . ."

"Where he risked being shot," I said, accurately if somewhat insensitively.

"Yes," she said. "Exactly. But Tyler's father finally convinced me. He said, 'He has something he truly wants to do. A calling. We should be behind him one hundred percent.'"

And so they were.

Tyler met Brittany while he was at Utah Valley University. He'd entered because he graduated from high school at seventeen, and you couldn't join the police academy until you were twenty. So he enrolled, took some criminal justice and journalism classes, and dropped out, with only a few credits left to earn for the year, the minute he turned twenty. Then he entered the academy.

Brittany had grown up in Utah and Las Vegas. Her mom's a Mormon but her biological dad, Kenny, is a Lutheran, and she grew up with the same kind of live-and-let-live attitude regarding religious faith that Tyler did. Brittany's parents divorced, and her biological dad lives in Iowa today, but he still comes out to visit his daughter and her family. "There's pretty good feelings all around," Tyler told me.

But Brittany's childhood hadn't been perfect. At the time Tyler met her, her parents were divorced, and there was the usual fallout when a family breaks apart. Tyler married her when he was twenty, and she was just sixteen.

"Sixteen, huh?" I said to Brittany on the phone one day, after Tyler suggested I give her a call to get her perspective on things.

"So was life really terrible at your house when Tyler came along?"

"No," Brittany said, clearly looking carefully for the right words and also looking to avoid the wrong ones. "It wasn't terrible. It was just . . . a hard time."

"And Tyler noticed that?"

"Oh yeah."

"So," I said, half-jokingly because it was so obvious, "I'm getting the feeling Tyler was always something of a 'rescuer.'"

Brittany laughed. "Yeah, you could say that."

Tyler officially became an officer on June 5, 2006. He was twenty-one. His first day on the job was a memorable one.

"So it's my first day as a fully instated member of the Spanish Fork Police Department," Tyler told me. "I'm a cop. I knew Brittany was proud of me. I knew the rest of my family was too—including my mom. My dad really got her around to the idea that if your kid has something he wants to do in life, it's a blessing. So she was behind me one hundred percent, too, and I wanted to make her proud. That first day, Brittany and the baby waved me out the door like it was 1942 and I was going off to fight the Nazis. Needless to say, I wanted to make her proud, too.

"So I get to the station and we go out on patrol, me and this other officer, a sergeant in the department. I was a rookie, out on his first ride, and I was beyond nervous. I asked the sergeant things like, 'What do I do at this next intersection? Do I take a left?' The sergeant said, 'If you want to. It's up to you.' It was a crazy sensation. I was behind the wheel of a patrol car, and there's your town all around you and it's your job to protect it.

You don't expect what that's going to feel like, how disorienting it is."

"Okay," I said. "You're driving around. What next?"

"In just a couple of minutes, we get a call."

"Is that unusual?"

"Yeah," Tyler said. "I mean, kind of. It's like fishing. You can drop your line in the water and get a bite, or you can wait five hours. There's no telling. But that day, right off the bat we get this call on the radio: '6J24, can you take a possible 1085 Echo?'

"*Echo* means someone's dead. I can't believe it. I pick up the radio and tell them we're responding. The address isn't far away. I hit the switch for the siren and the button for lights just under it, and I start going. It's the first time I've driven a car with lights and siren, and I'm not used to how cars just get out of my way. I went into a kind of tunnel vision, just not wanting to make a wrong turn with the sergeant there in the car with me."

Five minutes later, they pulled up at the house, a one-story rambler-style building not all that different from the one Tyler grew up in.

"We get out of the car, and I've already sweated through my shirt. There's a lady in front of the house, and she just says, 'He's out back.' We head around, and there's this regular-looking yard with a pretty big tree in it. Big enough that I figured it was probably there before the house went up. There's a long, thick, horizontal branch, and a guy hanging from it."

"What kind of rope was he hanging from?" I asked.

"Oh, just . . . ordinary brown hardware-store rope. We walk up to the guy. He's just a couple inches off the ground, just hanging there, not moving. He's wearing shorts and a Looney Tunes T-shirt. Like, it's the last day of his life, and that's what he's wearing. I don't know why, but that detail just freaked me out a little more than I already was. The sergeant tells me to check his pulse, so I take the guy's wrist. It's cold, like a frog. There's nothing. I tell the sergeant so, and he heads back to the front of the house, leaving me there standing next to this guy. The guy's mouth was slightly open, and he was wearing wire-rim glasses, and you could see that behind them his eyes were bugging out a little bit. But basically he just looked normal."

Out front another vehicle pulled up and an EMT came around and listened to the man's heart. The man was indeed dead. The sergeant came back around, too.

"The sergeant says, 'Hey, this is your first call so I'll take the report, but hang around.'"

"He said, 'hang around,' huh?" I asked.

"Yeah," Tyler said. "He knew what he was doing. He's a good guy. It wasn't like he was trying to make me suffer. He was just basically saying: 'Welcome to it. This is what being a police officer is all about.' So I just stood there next to this guy, trying not to get any more wigged out than I already was. The sergeant came back again in a little bit, and I guess I looked worse than when he left because he said, 'You look like you need to sit down.' I probably looked about the same as the guy hanging from the tree at that point. Anyhow, that was the first time I got it."

"Got what?"

"That flu feeling. It's what I always get in situations like that. Still today. All officers react differently to ugly situations.

Bodies, violence, blood . . . the smell of blood especially. It gets to you. Some guys don't show a thing, but they feel it, too, or at least most of them do. One guy in our department, every time he gets called to a bad situation, a bad traffic accident or a shooting or whatever, he loses it, just pukes his guts up. Every time. He's a good officer. We kid him about it, but we all understand. Everyone does something different. With me, it's that flu feeling. It's like I just get the worst flu you can imagine, instantly."

That night, Tyler came home from his first big day on the job to a hug from Brittany. She asked him how his day at work went.

Tyler gave her a simple answer. "Honey," he said, "I don't think I can do this job."

But Tyler returned the next day, and the next, and before long he discovered that he loved being a cop just as much as he had always dreamed he would. There were always bad situations, ugly ones, and sometimes downright dangerous ones. But the basic feeling Tyler usually came home with was that he had spent his day at a job where he had made a difference—made things a little better for at least one or two people, and sometimes a whole lot more than that.

"There has been some really nice stuff," he told me. "Incredible stuff. About four years ago, me and Harward were on patrol when we got a call that a six-year-old boy had collapsed on an elementary school playground. We got out of the car and found the kid lying by a jungle gym on the playground, on the grass, stone still, his face purple, and no breath. The chief of our unit was there, and he'd been administrating CPR but with no result.

We had an adult defibrillator with us. But twelve is the minimum age for an adult defibrillator. Use it on a six-year-old, and you risk basically blowing his heart up."

"So what happened?"

"Well, I had to make a decision, obviously. I figured, this may kill him, but he's pretty much dead already. So I lay the grips on the kid's rib cage, shout 'Clear!' and Harward turns on the juice. The charge blasted the kid three inches into the air."

And, as it happened, back to life. On the operating table later that day, surgeons discovered the child had a heart condition. No one had known anything about it until that moment on the playground when he'd simply collapsed in the middle of playing a game.

"I run into that kid from time to time," Tyler said. "He's doing great, and Spanish Fork being a small town I run into his mom, too. I don't know. I guess it might sound corny, but that's the kind of stuff I became an officer for. Not to be a hero, but to feel that sense that yeah, I made a difference today."

"So why did you do it?" I asked.

"Do what?" asked Tyler.

"Put that mechanism on him. The kid was six. The device wasn't safe for kids younger than twelve. What if you'd killed him?"

Tyler thought for a moment.

"Well, you have to remember that he was basically dead already. I mean, he wasn't breathing. His face was purple. He had about a minute or two before there wouldn't be any option left at all. Plus . . ."

Tyler hesitated a moment more.

"Plus what?" I said.

"There was just something that told me to do it. That it was okay."

That "just something" came up a lot with Tyler. Like most police officers, he got used to paying attention to what his intuition told him. He would go inside, listen, and act on what he heard.

"So who's telling you that stuff?" I asked.

Again there was a silence. Then Tyler, a Mormon, told me, an East Coaster almost completely ignorant about what real Mormon life is like, something I didn't know.

"Your guardian angel?" I threw out.

"Yeah," said Tyler. "I think you could say that."

"So," I asked, "do you believe you have a guardian angel?"

"Oh yeah," Tyler said.

"Is that something that Mormons believe—that people have guardian angels?"

"Oh sure, it's one of the main teachings. You learn it really early, and it sticks."

"So," I said, "when you were, like, ten, if you needed guidance with some problem, you'd turn to your guardian angel?"

"Sure."

"Is that what keeps you out of trouble today?"

"Yeah, I'd say so. I think I'd have to say yeah."

I knew that though angels are a nonnegotiable part of Christianity as a whole, not all Christians believed in guardian angels. I knew that Catholics did and that a lot of Protestants and Evangelicals didn't. But I was not really interested in that. What I was interested in was that Tyler lived an extremely chal-

lenging life, in which he had to make fast decisions all the time.
Tyler's day-to-day life was not cozy and abstract. He could be
killed any old time. His life was serious. He saw a lot of suffering, a lot of death, a lot of ugly, ugly things. How did he manage
it? That was what interested me. And with this piece of information, I thought I had another clue.

So all told, Tyler loved his job. All told, it was what he
thought it was going to be. Not all peaches and cream, but not
all garbage and misery either. But somewhere along the line—
about five years into his ten years on the force—something
started to change.

"I went from loving my job," Tyler said, "to hating it. In
the beginning, I'd figured: you show the people you deal with
respect, and they respect you back. Of course, if you're struggling to put someone in a choke hold because he's drunk and
disorderly, he's not going to have a lot of nice things to say to
you at the time. But I've had more than one guy who I've dealt
with when they were all messed up on something—drugs or
alcohol or whatever—and later, when everything was straight-
ened out and the guy's paid his fines or done his month of jail
or probation or whatever it is, he'll come and find me and tell
me that he appreciated how I dealt with him. He'll say, like, 'I
know I was pretty messed up, and giving you a challenge. You
could have smashed my head against the pavement, something
like that. But you didn't. I just want you to know I appreciate
that.'"

"Wow, that's happened?" I said, for some reason surprised
at this idea.

"Oh yeah, a bunch of times."

"That's pretty nice that someone would do that. That they'd see your side of things and make that effort."

"Oh yeah," Tyler said. "It definitely is. But . . . "

"But what?"

"But in the last five years, things have just done a complete one-eighty. I hate to say it, but basically I don't like my job now. It's like something's changed. And not just here either, not just with me. Now you turn on the news and you see five cops who've beat the crap out of some guy for no reason, or even killed him."

Tyler paused, knowing he was in a zone where he could say something he didn't quite mean, where he might end up rethinking what he said later and wishing he'd put it differently. He's not a complicated guy, but in a funny way, he *is* a complicated guy, and in the course of trying to get a handle on how his mind works, I've come to realize that there really and truly is a certain *something else* that he turns to when he's out in the field, even when he's not fully aware that he's doing it. He goes inside, and—without really even knowing he's doing it—he asks something inside him what to do. Then he comes back out and does it. I can sense him doing that now with me.

"I mean," Tyler continued, "there's always been those cops. Cops who'll say, 'Oh boy, we got this guy on a DUI and he's giving us some mouth.' There's plenty of guys like that outside the force, and there's some guys like that in the force, too, no question. You know they became cops because it's a great way to boss people around or beat them up and get paid for it.

"But the thing is, there's way less of those than the good ones. I mean, just way less. But these days at least, it seems like those kinds of cops are the ones drawing all the attention. Even though there's thousands of other cops who aren't like that at all, who joined up for good reasons. The right reasons. It's like four jerks somewhere in South Texas can be officially appointed by the media to stand for what all cops are like. I feel that every day. I'll be driving around in my squad car now, and someone will just flip me off."

"For what?" I asked.

"For nothing!" Tyler said, seemingly freshly amazed at the fact of it. "Just because I'm a cop, and cops are the bad guys now. Well, that is unless someone needs you. Then you're okay for a while. But even that's frustrating because there's so much going on these days with people. You'll get called to some house where a guy's flipping out because he found out his wife's been cheating on him, and you'll come in, and it's like everyone will turn and look at you and basically say: 'Okay, you're here. Fix this.' And, you know, you can't. You wouldn't believe some of the situations cops get called to these days. Family stuff. Psychological stuff. Stuff there should be other people to handle, professionals in those areas. But there aren't. Not anymore. Not like there used to be when there was money for that kind of stuff. And sure, of course you want to help. But you can't, at least beyond calming the situation down or whatever. There's just so much in life you can't fix these days. If you want to learn that fast, become a police officer."

I sympathized with that desire to fix the world and the knowledge that you can't—that you can barely fix anything. It made me think of a new question.

"What's the most frustrating type of case you get called on?" I asked. "Like, the worst *I-can't-fix-this* situation?"

"Oh, that's easy," said Tyler. "The sex cases. The sex cases will just drive you nuts."

At first I figured Tyler was talking about prostitution—that maybe there was some section of Spanish Fork with a red-light area, and he had to go back every night and deal with the same people.

But it turned out he was not talking about that.

"The abusers. They're what really get to me. We get called to a lot of home abuse cases. Situations where a dad or a stepdad is abusing one of his kids, or more than one. Taking advantage of them sexually. It's brutal. You take the kids away, but you don't know for sure if it'll hold, if they'll end up back in that house. It just makes you feel so powerless."

"What are the worst ones you've had in that department?"

"Easy again," Tyler said. "The elders. They're the worst. They're what really get you."

Once again, as an East Coaster, I didn't understand the reference. "Who are the elders?"

"The elders of the LDS," Tyler said, and at first I had to stop and recall what *LDS* even meant. Then I remembered: Latter-Day Saints. Tyler was talking about Mormon elders who abused their kids. I'm used to the controversy surrounding the Catholic clergy in recent years, and I of course know that this kind of thing happens among Evangelical churches, basically all kinds of institutions everywhere, and how much heartbreak it causes the members of these churches, both clergy and laypeople, who believe and who struggle with the realization that someone of their faith could do such evil. But somehow this was still surprising news to me.

"Does that happen a lot?"

"No, no," said Tyler. "Not at all when you look at the big pic-ture. I really want to emphasize that, because I love my faith and I love the people in it. I mean, Mormons are just like every other faith that way, or I guess every other faith—I'm no expert obvi-ously. But it seems to me that in any religion there are always a few bad apples, and just like in the police world, sometimes those bad apples work hard to get to the top of the heap, because that's where they can do what they want and have as few people above them to stop them from it. Ninety-nine point nine percent of Mormons are the nicest people you could ever hope to meet, and that goes for the elders, too. It's just like any other church, any other institution. There's just the bad ones is all. And it only takes dealing with a handful of cases like that to make you won-der. To shake your faith in this stuff."

By *this stuff*, I took it that Tyler basically meant "the world." It was the old, old question: If there's a God, how could he have set things up this way?

"Yeah," I said. "The world today can shake your faith in anything." And, of course, I meant it.

One case in particular stuck in Tyler's mind. He and another officer were called over to the house of a prominent local Mor-mon elder. A report had come in that he had regularly been mo-lesting his two daughters, nine and eleven. Tyler knocked on the man's door, and the man answered it. He asked Tyler if he could come back some other time. He was very busy, because he was preparing his talk for the next day—a Sunday—when he was to preach at his local congregation.

The combination of hardened experience and stubborn innocence I'd seen so often before in Tyler once again came to the fore. I could hear in his voice not just his rage but his sheer incredulity at the situation.

"Here's this guy, busy writing out this sermon that's going to tell everybody how to live upright in the eyes of the Lord. And meanwhile he's regularly been abusing these two girls who aren't even teenagers yet. It just makes your head spin. We charged him, took him in, and he got what he deserved. But it sticks with you."

"Yeah," I said. "Evil will do that. I recently learned something about one of the higher-ups in my elementary school back in the seventies—the guy who administered the discipline, the guy you made sure you steered clear of because he was really strict. He was like the original authority figure for me—the guy that, to this day, I still associate with what *authority* means. Well, it turns out that all the years I was at that school, he was molesting the female students. In the end, it was a girl in my grade who ended up bringing him to justice."

America started out as a country that was going to try to address this evil element in humankind—this fallen, corrupt nature that Adam and Eve's sin pins on us—in a new way. America was to be the place where the New Man was to be born—a being who lived beyond the sins of the past and was directed toward the hope of the future.

What this hope eventually turned into was what high school and college teachers call the "myth of progress." Our love of progress, our need to feel that we are "moving forward," as everyone likes to say today, is based on the notion that we can find a way out of human corruption. Like the Babylonians who built

the ziggurats or the men who built the Tower of Babel, we believe that progress in itself is a kind of stairway to heaven.

Yet look what that so-called progress has led to these days.

As a kid, Tyler had had an easy time with progress. Like
most Americans, he liked the idea on principle. But for ten years
his work on the force had been slowly, steadily—you might even
say mercilessly—grinding away at that idea. He was returning
home at night with dead eyes; when Brittany saw them she
knew what kind of day Tyler had had. She didn't even bother
asking, as she knew that in those moments, she was doing him
a favor in just staying quiet. On nights like that, Tyler would
be torn between his desire to spill his guts, tell Brittany every
last ghastly aspect of whatever case he'd worked on, or to shield
her from it. To take a shower, change into fresh clothes, have a
couple of beers, and declare the day closed.

But those doors rarely stayed closed, badly as Tyler wanted
them to. They swung open, and out came the images, the sounds,
and the smells. As any police officer, and anyone who's been
in battle, will likely tell you, smells, just in themselves, can be
mysteriously terrifying, mysteriously panic-inducing. It almost
seemed to Tyler sometimes as if they had minds of their own.

Faith is a language: one that each of us learns, or doesn't
learn, from others or just by ourselves. No one goes through the
world not wondering what the world is about—what kind of
place it is. But some wonder more than others. And at a certain
point in his ten years on the Spanish Fork Police Force, Tyler
began to realize that faith was a language he didn't fully speak.
Not well enough. Not well enough to handle what he saw each
day. He may still have had a guardian angel, and he may still

have relied on it to see him through each day, but his contact with that being was growing ever more tenuous, and the more tenuous it got, the more lost, the more defeated Tyler felt as he faced the evil of the world.

Gradually, so slowly that Tyler didn't even realize it at first, something inside him started to shift. The daily ugliness started wearing on him in a way it hadn't during his first years on the force. He'd come home feeling dirty, and the dirt wouldn't wash off. His guardian angel, perhaps overtaxed by the sheer amount of daily material it was tasked with shielding Tyler from, was letting way too much slip past.

In the two years leading up to the episode at Spanish Fork Bridge, two incidents occurred that undermined Tyler's attitude toward his job with a new kind of power. They made him start questioning things—things about life—that he hadn't thought about heavily since he was a kid.

"This'll sound dumb," Tyler said to me, "but these two things that happened, they started me in on more than just having problems with my job. They started me in on having problems with life. With what it's about. With whether it's about anything at all."

While Tyler and Brittany's house was being built, they went to live with Brittany's mom, Shelly, and her stepdad, Kirt, in Springville, a town not too far from Spanish Fork.

"It was June 2013. Brit and the kids and I had just got home, and we were unpacking when I got a call on my cell. It was the lieutenant down at the station. He told me there'd just been a report of a deceased male and a deceased child found at a home. I was coming up on my first ever cycle as detective, so I figured the lieutenant thought that even though I was still technically off duty, this would be a good first case for me to work. I wouldn't be the lead investigator, but I'd follow along, keep my eyes open, and just get a handle on working a case in that capacity."

Tyler and a partner drove to the residence and learned more details. A woman had come home to the house where she and her brother were living with his two-year-old son, following a breakup between him and the child's mom. The sister found a message taped to the back door, written in her brother's hand.

"The note," Tyler told me, "said what to do with his property, who to leave this and that to, not to go inside, and to call the police."

The sister went in anyhow. The living room was in complete disarray, lamps knocked over, and there were what looked like blood marks on the walls. She went upstairs to the room where her two-year-old nephew slept and found him laid out on his mattress on the floor, as he would usually be. The child was wearing just a diaper, and he was dead. The sister could see blood in his hair and bruises, heavy and dark like storm clouds, on the pale skin of the boy's back and arms.

In a panic, the woman searched the rest of the house. There was a basement workshop where her brother spent a lot of time, and it was there that she found him. He was dead on the floor from a gunshot to the head, the gun he'd used still in his hand.

"When I got there," Tyler said, "the place was taped off and ready for investigation, but still not too many people had gone in. I met with the other investigators and the lieutenant. He told me we were going to go through the house and I was going to videotape it. Once the search warrant arrived, I got on my marshmallow suit and went in."

"Marshmallow suit?" I asked.

"That's what we call the hazmat suits they make you wear in situations like that. It minimizes your impact on the scene, and it keeps you safe from any blood or other materials that might be present. It's bulky and you feel like an astronaut, but you got to wear them. So we walked through and I filmed, going from room to room, focusing in on every detail I felt might be of importance. I walked into the kid's bedroom and there was the mattress on the floor, and the kid. You could see he was heavily bruised from being beaten—that that was the cause of his death. But the thing was, it came home to me all of a sudden that all the blood marks that were on the walls of the house— they were there from the kid being thrown against them. There were a bunch of mostly empty vodka bottles down in the living room by the TV, so it became pretty clear what had probably happened. The guy had gotten just crazy drunk and thrown his kid all around the house, bouncing him off the walls like a doll. There was blood on the kitchen table so he'd probably slammed him down there a couple of times as well. Then when he'd finished—or maybe he passed out for a while and woke up back in his senses—he did the only thing he figured he could do. He took his kid up to bed and laid him down, put him to bed. Then he wrote that note for the door to protect his sister from seeing what had happened, and went down to the cellar and took his own life."

"So," I said, "a man under enormous psychological pressure snaps, and gets taken over by a rage that knows no limits. He becomes someone else basically. Then the rage passes, and the man, in a pathetic last gesture of affection for the boy he killed, lays him down to rest, just like it's a normal night. Then he goes down to his basement and commits the last—the only—action available to him."

"Yup," said Tyler in the same paradoxically profound yet gee-whiz way he has. "That's pretty much it."

"That's about the most tragic and sad story I've ever heard."

"Yeah," said Tyler.

Then, to lighten the mood, I said, "I guess I'd make quite a detective myself."

Tyler laughed and said, "Yup, you sure would."

But it turned out there was more to the story. The next morning, after a full night without sleep investigating the crime scene, Tyler went up to Salt Lake City and watched the child's autopsy. Doctors placed the boy on a table, cut his chest down the center, clipped open the rib cage, examined and removed the tiny, orderly placed organs from within his chest cavity, then peeled off the rest of the child's skin.

"These guys," Tyler said, "I knew they were professionals. You do anything enough, you get used to it. But watching a boy pretty much the same age as my son get gutted and skinned like a deer—it was tough."

Tyler went home and grabbed his kids and hugged them. He hugged Brittany, too. It only took one look at his face for Brittany to get the gist of what he'd been up to all night and all morning.

"She can read me the minute I walk in the door," Tyler said. "My face, my skin color . . . she says I get this kind of stare, and when she sees it, she knows I'm mostly not there, that a good slice of me is absent, and that I can't come back even though I want to, and that she just has to wait a while."

That day, Brittany had long since begun to wonder just how much more of her husband his job was going to take away from her. But over the next few months, the memory of the incident faded, or seemed to fade.

Then came the case that changed everything.

CHAPTER 6

---❦---

A Voice from Somewhere Else

[Lying on her bed crying and alone, she suddenly felt the touch of a hand on her arm.]

It startled me a bit but I just kept on crying. And then this voice said, "What's the matter? Why are you crying? What is it? Tell me."

And I just said, "I'm sorry. I'm really, really sorry."

And she said, "What are you sorry for?"

And I said, "I'm sorry for my reaction to my mother when I was young."

She then said, "Is that all? Anyone in your family would have reacted in the same way."

At that I opened my eyes to look at her. And standing there was this huge being in a brilliant white light. It was the most beautiful thing I've ever seen in my whole life.

—FROM *SPIRITUAL ENCOUNTERS WITH UNUSUAL LIGHT PHENOMENA* BY MARK FOX

ANGELS DO NOT, of course, manifest only by sight. At *Angels on Earth*, I spoke regularly to people who had been nudged by angels, whispered to by angels, and presented with hints by angels. The hints, in particular, weren't always totally convincing, though they clearly were to the people who had experienced them. Say your husband dies. For years he'd been trying to make a tree in your backyard blossom in spring, and it never has. Yet the spring after his death, lo and behold, the tree he had worked so hard to make flourish has exploded into blossom. What does this mean? It all depends on whom you ask. A daughter is visiting the grave of a grandparent who collected butterflies. Out of the blue, as she is sitting by the graveside, a butterfly lands on the gravestone. When the young woman rises to leave, the butterfly rises from the gravestone and follows her all the way back to her car. What does this mean? Once again, arguing about the answer is fruitless. To the person who has experienced it, it means volumes. To someone not disposed to the reality of angels, it means nothing. All one can say in regard to stories of this nature is: to each his own.

*All five senses can play a part in
angel encounters.*

All five senses can play a part in angel encounters, as is witnessed by the number of saints who have had mysterious, heavenly scents associated with them, especially with their bodies after death, which the Catholic church maintains have remained incorruptible for days, weeks, or even years. Angels also heal people who are hopelessly beyond healing, at least according to their doctors. People at death's door have been brought back to glowing health after an encounter with what they say is an angel. One can doubt the reason such people give for their miraculous recovery, but the recoveries themselves number in the thousands. Here, for example, is a story from the French investigative reporter Pierre Jovanovic's *An Inquiry into the Existence of Guardian Angels*, which I have edited for length.

I remember hearing the doctors talk at my bedside, and they were saying, No hope for this one. We'll try to stabilize him to make him comfortable and then send him home. What else can we do? They gave me a bottle of oxygen. I couldn't take a step without that bottle. A little later, new problems came along. I became hypoglycemic as well as hyperglycemic. Then I began to fall into a coma regularly, and lose my memory, weight, and so on. I went from bad to worse.

Before that I went to mass every Sunday like everybody else, [but] God was not of primary importance. Money was the main thing, and I'd always put money before God. I loved money, but money didn't give me back my lungs. Everything I'd saved went for medical care. At one point I even believed that we were going to lose our house. Then one day in church during a Mass, I had the feeling that it was my last. I felt I couldn't go on. Leaving the church after Mass, a woman saw me with my bottle of oxygen and said to me "Why don't you go to Lubbock in Texas?" I'd never heard of it. So-called apparitions of the Virgin occurred there. I answered, "Sure, why not?" I had nothing to lose at that point. Oddly enough, I had no bad spells during the trip from Kansas to Texas. I found that really remarkable. But once we reached Lubbock, my body fell apart. I was so weak from losing weight that I couldn't climb stairs. We went to Mass in the evening and then went back to the motel. Suddenly I was hungry. Terribly hungry. A hunger like none I had ever known. I ate day and night, about every two hours. I had to eat and eat and eat. Next day we stayed in church all day to say the rosary. I still had no bad spells. It was more and more miraculous. In the chapel, towards 5:30 PM, I reached the last rosary and this time I prayed for Mary to intercede with Jesus in my favor because I wanted to live and I had four children. As I began the Crucifixion, a woman dressed in white appeared beside me. She was magnificent. I remember that I didn't see her feet. Suddenly I felt a hand on my shoulder. I turned, but there was no one but my wife and me in the chapel. But the hand was still there. I said to myself, "I've lost half my brain, and this time I'm really going crazy," and I said to my wife, "Listen, take me on back, I think I'm not well." In fact, I believed that I'd gone mad. As I crossed the threshold of the chapel, I passed out. Later, when I came to, this man explained that he was convinced that I was going to die on the spot, so he rushed to the front for some holy water and sprinkled me with it from head to toe. I got up without thinking, took my reservoir of oxygen and walked toward the church, and at that moment I realized that I could walk alone. Usually fatigue overcame me after a few steps, and I now could climb stairs without a problem. Gradually something told me I no longer needed oxygen, and I removed the tube. A priest saw me and rushed toward me. He forced me to put it back, saying I must do exactly as usual. I did replace the tube but cut off the oxygen. I recovered completely on October 9, 1988, the lungs as well as the brain. When I got home to Kansas, the doctor gave me a breathing test and the needle oscillated between 575 and 600 when before I never went over 350. One month later I hit 675. The doctor told me, "It's impossible." But I was breathing perfectly and he saw the dial. Nobody could get over it; it was as if they refused to believe their own eyes. When the doctor looked at the X-rays he had a shock: no trace of spots, problems, nothing. I was like new.

Angels are great—if typically quite terse—dispensers of advice. People paralyzed by a particular life situation will hear a sentence or two, delivered by no one that they can see, that suddenly makes them view their situation in an entirely new light. Likewise, as in the Cokeville siege, people in extremis can receive quick, no-nonsense directives that end up saving their lives.

How can one hear a voice that isn't there? Paranoid schizophrenics sometimes spend decades listening to inner voices, often very negative ones. For the people experiencing such a voice, it is as real as one they might hear from a flesh-and-blood person. The brain has the ability to create such illusions, and this is a fact that no one argues about. The questions arise when these voices don't speak random gibberish or trivial insults, but deliver true and valuable information that ends up benefiting the hearer.

Such advice, spoken by invisible beings, was extremely common in the ancient world. No one questioned it. Ever since Julian Jaynes published his revolutionary book *The Origin of Consciousness in the Breakdown of the Bicameral Mind* in 1976, the idea that ancient people lived in a genuinely different world than ours and how it changes—or doesn't change—over the centuries have been topics of heated discussion by students of consciousness. What kind of world did the ancients live in, according to Jaynes? In brief, a world in which the gods—via statues, or visibly, or by means of apparitions—spoke to the ancients, not metaphorically but actually. How could this be? Jaynes, who never left the materialist model of the universe completely behind, suggested that it had to do with a bifurcation between the left and right brains, which allowed people to actually hear voices coming from their right brain and experience those voices as coming from outside of them.

However sharply they were heard, most modern psychologists would say that these voices and visions emerged from the "unconscious" of these ancient peoples. But what *is* the unconscious? Is it just some spot located in the brain, or is it the key to a new vision of the brain in which it acts not as the producer of consciousness, but as a kind of antenna and condenser, taking our real, true, full consciousness, which we experience completely only when out of the body, and crushing it down so that it is able to focus on the day-to-day demands of life in the material world? All too often, the word *unconscious* shows up as a blanket term to cover any phenomenon that contemporary science/ psychology has no explanation for. But it's not up to the task. Like it or not, things are simply more complicated than that.

Is it possible that actual intelligences could exist beyond the boundaries of the physical brain, in a world beyond the boundaries of the physical world?

When an individual hears voices with perfect clarity (whether that individual is a saint like Joan of Arc or the unfortunate inmate of a mental institution), it is by no means always easy to dismiss the phenomenon as "mental illness," even though many contemporary scientists would like to do so. If the unconscious is located solely in the brain of the individual, how can it be that these voices often deliver information that the individual in question could not possibly otherwise have known? It's an established, but little commented-on, fact that telepathy has been proved. Countless statistical tests, many of them conducted at the Rhine Research Center at Duke University, have demonstrated that the faculty exists to the satisfaction of most scientists—the ones who don't accept it usually being die-hard materialists who refuse it on what are essentially dogmatic rather than scientific grounds. When scientists who don't believe that consciousness can exist beyond the body want to debunk an instance of communication from "beyond," a common strategy is to "explain" the event by saying that telepathy was involved. Say an individual dies before he or she has been allowed to deliver a crucial piece of information. The classic examples of this often involve wills that have been rewritten. Somehow or other, information appears that allows people still living to uncover the rewritten will from whatever drawer or cabinet it has been placed in. There are dozens of such stories, and they are quite simply impossible to explain from a completely empirical standpoint. So it is that the solution for individuals who refuse to believe that information can come from beyond the brain is to invoke telepathy. Obviously, the debunker will say, someone living was aware of the whereabouts of the will, and the person who learned of it simply picked this information up telepathically. There is no need to fall into such traps as the illusion that life continues beyond the body. Chalk it up to telepathy, and the problem is solved.

Yet how much does such an explanation really solve? For if telepathy is an established fact, doesn't this knock the foundations out from underneath all strictly materialist explanations of unusual phenomena? Far from being a tool that helps discount the reality of the invisible world, the fact of telepathy is instead just one more suggestion that that world really exists.

Sometimes seemingly telepathic communications—communications that result from some function of the brain that transcends its physicality—come not via audible voices, but simple feelings: feelings whose origin cannot be explained but which end up providing crucial and often lifesaving instructions to the individual who experiences them.

In *An Inquiry into the Existence of Guardian Angels*, Jovanovic retells this story of a professional photographer:

> *One night in October 1991 in Los Angeles, I was following a friend's car, and we stopped for a red light at the intersection of Robertson on Burton. The light turns green, the car*

in front of me starts up and turns left. I had taken my foot off the brake and my car started forward, but—and I don't know why—I stopped when I had absolutely no reason to. One second later a car came barreling up from my right like a rocket, doing maybe sixty, carried off my bumper in a screech of torn metal, did a 180, rolled over, smashed into a parked car to its right and came to rest upside-down. If I'd made the turn I was about to make, with that car coming on at that speed, I'd unquestionably have been gravely injured or killed. I have no idea why my foot hit the brake, as if by instinct, when I had no reason to stop, none at all, and I was already in the intersection. And I hadn't seen or heard anything.

The ancient world spoke of the daimon or genius—a personal spirit that guided individuals through their lives, dispensing advice at pivotal moments. In early Christianity, this "daimonic" voice became one of two things. It could be the individual's good or guardian angel, who, like a producer behind the scenes at a live TV show, whispered just the right information in an individual's ear when it was needed. Or the daimon could become a "demon," a not-so-trustworthy voice that spoke to the individual as well, but not to help him or her, but instead lead him or her into trouble. All the cartoons I grew up with in which Bugs Bunny or Daffy Duck suddenly faced a conundrum and a little angel appeared on one shoulder and a little devil on the other, each offering conflicting advice, trace back to these ancient ways of thinking about angels and demons.

But cartoons are not the only legacy of those ancient times. These experiences, and the beings behind them, are still with us. Angels are manifestations, unquestionably real to those who encounter them, of a world larger, better, and infinitely more beautiful, intelligent, and anchored in the reality of God than ours is. The existence of angels drives home the fact that we are not lost and alone in this modern flatland of materialism, but come from, and will return to, another, better place. That is the most important message that the angel brings in our time—or any time—and limiting all the evidence of this to the brain is a popular, but ultimately losing, proposition.

The existence of angels drives home the fact that we are not lost and alone in this modern flatland of materialism, but come from, and will return to, another, better place. That is the most important message that the angel brings in our time—or any time—and limiting all the evidence of this to the brain is a popular, but ultimately losing, proposition.

"Who is the third who walks always beside you?" This famous line, from T. S. Eliot's *The Waste Land*—the single most celebrated poem of the twentieth century—is loosely based on an actual event that occurred when the explorer Ernest Shackleton was crossing Elephant Island in Antarctica with a few of the remaining survivors of his crew after a disastrous attempt to conquer the South Pole. During this long, brutal, final leg of the explorer's journey back to civilization, he could not shake the feeling that there was an additional member of his group trekking across the ice with them: a member he could keenly sense, but which, when he turned to look for it, he could not see.

This event is, of course, also eerily reminiscent of the episode in the New Testament in which the disciples, walking to the town of Emmaus following the crucifixion, find themselves in the company of a mysterious stranger: a stranger whom they eventually recognize, not as an angel, but as the risen Christ.

During his historic 1927 one-man crossing of the Atlantic from the United States to Europe, aviator Charles Lindbergh had a similar experience. "Darkness set in about 8:15," wrote Lindbergh in his memoir *The Spirit of St. Louis*, "and a thin, low fog formed over the sea. . . . This fog became thicker and increased in height until within two hours I was just skimming the top of storm clouds at about ten thousand feet. Even at this altitude there was a thick haze through which only the stars directly overhead could be seen. There was no moon and it was very dark."

Deep into his trip and high above the empty Atlantic, Lindbergh began to grow groggy. In the age before automatic pilots, Lindbergh struggled to keep focused on his instrument panel and to keep his hands on the controls. To doze off even for a moment would mean death in the Atlantic below.

The isolation and weariness made Lindbergh meditate on the intimate closeness of death. But as the miles of open sea passed by beneath him, Lindbergh increasingly felt that he was not alone. Behind him, in the fuselage of the plane, he sensed the presence of human forms, transparent and weightless.

"While I'm staring at the instruments," he wrote, "the fuselage behind me becomes filled with ghostly presences—vaguely outlined forms, transparent, moving, riding weightless with me in the plane."

Lindbergh felt no fear at the appearance of these "friendly, vaporlike shapes," who spoke with "human voices." In fact, he sensed they were there to help.

In words that echo Ralph Waldo Emerson's famous lines about becoming a "transparent eye-ball" during a moment of heightened insight he experienced, Lindbergh writes: "I see them [the angelic figures] as clearly as though in my normal field of vision. There's no limit to my sight—my skull is one great eye, seeing everywhere at once.

"First one and then another presses forward to my shoulder to speak above the engine's noise, and then draws back among the group behind. They're neither intruders nor strangers. It's more like a gathering of family and friends after years of separation."

When we travel to the edge of the known world (a project increasingly difficult these days), we seem to key our psyches to leave behind their ordinary prejudices, their ordinary filters for reality. We become open to seeing, hearing, and feeling realities that the all-too-familiar comforts (and disappointments) of our ordinary lives tend to block out. The same goes for tragic accidents. They knock us out of our ordinary mental framework. They shake us up, and in that moment of vulnerability, perceptions of the world beyond can occur. And these perceptions are frequently wonderful—so much so that the individual who has experienced them, once he or she has returned to conventional reality with all its sleepy-making familiarity, remembers them for years to come with a clarity that makes it seem as if they happened yesterday.

In 1933, mountain climber Francis Sydney Smythe was high on Mount Everest when he felt himself joined by a "strong and friendly" invisible companion. "In its company," Smythe wrote, "I could not feel lonely, neither could I come to any harm. It was always there to sustain me on my solitary climb up the snow-covered slabs. Now, as I halted and extracted some mint cake from my pocket, it was so near and so strong that instinctively I divided the mint into two halves and turned around with one half in my hand to offer it to my 'companion.'"

Theodora Ward, who includes this story in her book *Men & Angels*, also tells of a Scottish couple who was trailed by an "unseen presence" while crossing the Greenland ice cap. Ward makes the point that in the overwhelming majority of these encounters, the presence is specifically described as being friendly.

In a world where we are not permitted to take the supernatural seriously, the most common way for supernatural agencies to manifest is in our minds. When they do so, they translate themselves into feelings and impulses. As the pioneering contemporary psychologist and student of world mystical traditions Wilson Van Dusen has shown, the best place to find someone in contact with an angel or a devil currently is not a church, but a mental hospital. There, one may see people in active conversation with invisible agencies that anyone who has worked with such people knows are hard to dismiss as simple figments of the patient's imagination. As suggested earlier, some of these invisible entities are fantastically cruel. Like the beings that made Howard Storm miserable during his walk down the hospital hall, they often seem to take tremendous pleasure in tormenting their human victims. Other such beings, meanwhile, have better intentions but can cause damage as well when they show their subjects explosively vivid visions of the universe: visions so sweeping, so gorgeous, so vastly and terribly real, that the patient comes back from them either charged with vitality (that is, "mania" or "grandiosity" or "inflation" in today's psychological language) or with their circuits so thoroughly blown that when they talk they make no sense, and they are even less capable of interacting with, and getting along in, our ordinary, humdrum, angels-don't-exist world outside their barred windows than they were before. The examples of "outsider art" that have recently been receiving attention from the art community are, at their best, wonderfully persuasive of just how real these alternate universes, and the beings inhabiting them, can be for the individuals experiencing them.

Some of the greatest artists have been adamant about the "help" they have received from outside agencies in creating their works.

Some of the greatest artists have been adamant about the "help" they have received from outside agencies in creating their works. Charles Dickens famously said that he sometimes felt less like a novelist than a stenographer, as he struggled to write as fast as he could in order to keep up with what his characters said and did. Perhaps not coincidentally, Dickens's most beloved story, *A Christmas Carol*, features an angel: one who arrives at the last minute to educate a man of supreme selfishness on the benefits of being interested in others.

Where does artistic inspiration, especially of the kind artists like Dickens had, come from? If you are on the "intellectual" side of the schism between the "dumb" believers and the "smart" unbelievers that seems to divide our world ever more each day, your reaction is practically automatic. If you are on the other side of that schism—the of-course-God's-heavenly-angels-exist side—then you may accept the reality of angelic beings and their effect on us with a quickness, ease, and lack of surprise that is, in its way, just as insulting to the genuine truth of these beings as its dismissal by close-minded materialists. Neither of these two responses, it seems to me, is the right one. The spiritual world is huge, shocking, terrifying, and inspiring. To deny it is a mistake. To take it too much for granted is one as well.

To take the celebrated phrase attributed to Saint Paul, each of us lives and moves and has our being in the spiritual dimension, and people who claim no connection to this dimension are (to use a very old Arab analogy) like fish that claim no knowledge of water.

It may be that we live in a world where supernatural beings swarm around us at all times, just as Saint Paul very clearly thought we do. As writer Mark Booth has suggested in his books *The Secret History of the World* and its sequel *The Sacred History*, the great figures of history have always been in contact with invisible beings that affected their actions, charging them with tremendous force at one moment, weakening them hopelessly at others. History itself is in large part the story of the invisible world and its effects on this visible one that we stumble through every day, hopelessly thinking that we are fully in charge.

Does the invisible world exist? Do angels exist? Do you hate the word *angel* because it sounds stupid? Then use the word *devil* instead. Though I have no desire to get too close to them, I have come to see the use of devils. Though in far from the best way, they wake people up. They show us that the world we live in—the world of shopping malls and rental cars—hides another supernatural world behind it. Life, as Blake famously put it, is "twofold." The mundane world is actually but one part of a much fuller and more complete world, which contains far more within it than we can imagine. In a sense, the mundane is the outer layer or "crust" of reality. To see both the crust and the larger realm lying behind it is to see with twofold vision. When we shift to this kind of vision, we are right where we were before. But the world around us has suddenly become a much more rich and crowded place. Like Evie that day down in the Bahamas by that lonely outcropping of rock, we have put our face beneath the surface, and discovered that we are far from alone after all.

CHAPTER 7

A Presence in the Room

My grandmother . . . and her younger sister were in East-
bourne to visit my great-grandmother who was very ill and not
expected to live very long. Walking away from the house one
afternoon—and having found her very much at peace, though
quite obviously very poorly—they were discussing the situation
and, no doubt, preparing for the inevitable, when they both
stopped in their tracks and caught hold of one another, saying
"did you see that?" They both—independently—claimed to
have seen two shining winged people, who [they] were con-
vinced must have been angels, gently escorting a human away.
It was over in a second, but my grandma and aunty never for-
got this experience, as they heard on their way home that their
mum had died—at the precise moment they saw the angels . . .

—HEATHCOTE-JAMES, QUOTED IN *SPIRITUAL ENCOUNTERS WITH*

UNUSUAL LIGHT PHENOMENA BY MARK FOX

JOSH BOREN, THE next individual to step in Tyler's path and
rattle his sense of faith leading up to the crash at the Spanish

Fork Bridge, was a cop. He lived in Spanish Fork but worked in a station a few towns north. One night in January 2014, officers got a call to go to Boren's residence to do a welfare check on him, as he hadn't showed up for his graveyard shift the night before.

"I got called in to assist the detective in charge. There were a couple of cops there ahead of me, but I was one of the first on the scene. I was told to go over and help check out the house, collect evidence, and secure the area."

None of this jibed with my understanding of how police detective work happened. I was used to movies, where the cops show up first, then clear out when Bruce Willis and Al Pacino step onto the scene in their long coats and shiny black shoes and start figuring out what really went on.

"Yeah," Tyler said. "Turns out it doesn't really work like that. The basic detective stuff is just sketching the scene, taking in the evidence. All the officers do it, and that particular month, I was still on the roster. So we headed over to Boren's house, which isn't far from the Spanish Fork police station. I didn't know Boren, never met him. But I had friends who knew him. He was a regular cop, a good guy—that's what I heard. But it turned out that Boren's wife had been cheating on him. She'd kicked him out of their house, and that night he'd come over to see the kids, and there was a dispute of some kind.

"We pull up, and there's one other squad car there. We look through the windows, try to see what's going on inside, then we wait for the warrant to search. It comes in about half an hour, we get in our marshmallow suits, and we go in."

"What did you see?"

"On the ground floor, nothing much. A couple of lamps and

plants had been knocked over. There weren't any bodies or any-thing. But there were some spent bullet casings on the floor. In the kitchen, there was a staircase leading up to the main bed-room. Me and my partner, we go up the stairs. It's quiet. We weren't the first to go to the second floor, but I still didn't have a full idea of what we were walking into."

Tyler and his partner got to the top of the stairs and saw the doorway to the master bedroom just a few feet away. It was open. They walked in and saw a scene such as Tyler had never imag-ined. Not in his police work, and not in his worst nightmares.

As Tyler described it, I noted, not for the first time, that strange combination of innocence and experience in his voice. He was, it occurred to me, perhaps the most unique combina-tion of these qualities I'd ever come across. On one level, he sounded like a kid describing a basketball game. Yet at the same time, he talked with the authority and knowledge of someone who had seen, and done, a whole lot more than I will ever see or do, or could even imagine doing.

"In the room," Tyler said, "the first thing you see is the mas-ter bed. Boren's whole family is in it, or maybe I should say on it, as there's no sheets over them. But they're laid out as a fam-ily would be. There's the wife over on the far side, then two kids, his seven-year-old son, Josh, and his five-year-old, Haley, in between them. And then there's Boren. They're all dead. You could see where Boren had put a bullet in each of their heads, and through each of their hearts. Boren's still got the gun in his hand, a .45. So it was pretty clear what happened. Boren had killed his wife and kids, laid them down in bed, and then got in on his side and shot himself."

"So," I said, "he'd come over to visit the kids, and maybe some kind of argument had started up, and Boren had decided he wasn't accepting the new situation—wasn't digesting that his family had really and truly broken up, so he decided to keep them together in the only way he could think of."

"Yup, you could put it that way for sure," Tyler said, and we made a few more of the usual jokes about what a great detective I'd make. "But it probably didn't happen just like that, actually, because down the hall from the master bedroom was a smaller one, where Boren's wife's mom had been staying since the breakup, helping with the kids. We walked down and found her there. She was sitting in an easy chair, with some knitting in her hands. She'd been shot once, in the face, not in the heart and the head like the other ones. So Boren must have come in pretty fast for her to be just sitting there like that, like he'd just walked down the hall, shot her, then got back to the real business at hand. She'd been wearing eyeglasses, and you could see pieces of them driven back into her skull. You know that rule about how you never punch someone wearing glasses? Well, to me the fact that he'd just plugged her in the face like that, with her glasses on—to me it just gave me the idea that in his eyes she didn't fit into the family unit, that he didn't care about her the way he cared about the other ones."

"People really are developing some pretty strange ways of showing they care about each other these days," I said, to lighten the mood.

"Yeah," said Tyler, "I guess you could sure say that," and from his tone throughout this whole story I could tell that talking about it was bringing it all back for him, and that he was not over it.

"Anyhow," Tyler said, "that was just the start of the night. I was there for the next twelve hours. It was my job to sketch the scene, to note all the bullet marks, to collect the shells, all that. It's stuff I'd done a million times before, just rote. But being in that room . . . it got to me more than usual. The second I walked in and saw the bed, that flu feeling hit me like it never had before. It was like a freight train."

"How old did you say the Boren children were again?" I asked.

"The boy was seven; the girl was five," Tyler said.

"Pretty close to your kids' ages," I said.

"Yeah," Tyler said. "For months after that, I'd come home and sometimes, if it was late, Gracie and Gunnar would have gotten into bed with Brittany, and I'd look at them sleeping and the Boren bed would superimpose itself on the picture. There was a while when I couldn't get to sleep at all without taking some NyQuil, and I'd still wake up periodically through the night."

As Tyler described the rest of the evening to me—the forensic specialists crowding in, the men from the morgue, more cops from the station—I noticed that he kept going back to this one thing in particular that bothered him, that made the whole evening an extra heavy challenge to endure, even given all he had seen of death and tragedy by that point in his career.

"There was something in the room that night," Tyler said. "I don't know really how to explain it, other than that it was real, that I could feel it—that it was there, every bit as much as the furniture and the bodies and the other people. It was like a kind of force. A feeling that just made me sick at the pit of my stomach and made me want to run out of there."

Not wanting to lead him, but seeing pretty clearly where this was going, I tried a word out. "Was it a feeling of evil?"

"Yup. That was it. Just pure evil. It was so strong, and it was hanging over everything. There's only one thing that made me able to stand it, to not just bolt out of there."

"What was that?"

"At around two in the morning, I'm taking photos and talking with the other people in there. You try to keep the amount of people in the room in a scene like that down to a certain number or it turns into chaos. But it always gets crowded anyhow, and at this point there were six or seven people in the room, all trying to do their jobs without getting on top of each other. Anyhow, I'm standing by the bed, by those bodies, both looking at the children and trying not to look at the children, because every time I do I get another wave of that flu feeling shooting through me. And suddenly, I get this feeling around my legs. It sounds crazy, but I look down, and though I can't see anything, I just get this feeling, real and plain as day, that those two kids are there, at my legs, and they're hugging me."

"You can feel two kids hugging you around the knees through your marshmallow suit?" I asked.

"Yeah. I know it doesn't make any sense. But it's real. It's real and it just goes through me like a wave, a wave of love, even though I know that doesn't make any sense either, describing it that way."

"And you think it's those two kids?"

"I know it's those two kids," said Tyler. "And the thing, the most incredible thing about it, is that I can feel them, their feelings, and I realize they're not feeling bad for themselves. They're feeling bad for me, because they can tell that I'm in bad shape. They can see what all this is doing to me. And it's like I can feel them talking to me."

"What were they saying?" I asked.

"'It's all right,'" Tyler said. "They're telling me it's all right."

Thinking about Tyler's experience with the boy who'd been murdered by his single-dad father and the horror he encountered at the Boren house, it came home to me clearly that he was not simply complaining about what a tough job it is to be a police officer sometimes, or about how little appreciation police officers are getting these days. Those elements were there, but Tyler was not a whiner. From the very beginning of our conversations, I got the clear impression that he had not been a "poor me" kid, and was certainly not a "poor me" adult. He was telling me these stories, I realized, for two reasons. One was that like many, many others, he is clearly aware that something is wrong with America these days. All kinds of things that used to hold together in our society are no longer doing so. As he often said in our talks, "This world's going to hell in a handbasket," and he suffered daily frustration at seeing this fact and not being able to do anything about it.

The other, subtler thing he was trying to tell me was tied, somehow, to the first, and it had to do with that word that came up in the middle of his narrative of the Boren case.

"So what do you really think about good and evil?" I asked Tyler the next time we talked.

"What do you mean?" he said.

"I mean, in these stories you've been telling me, you've used very physical language to describe things that are essentially invisible. The kids hugging you—that's an obvious case. But the sense of evil that you got a taste of at that first house with the dead boy, and the overwhelming sense of it that you got at the Boren house. It makes me wonder what you think good and evil really are. Are they just abstractions, ways of talking about how people behave?"

Tyler was firm in his answer. There was no trace of "gee whiz" in his tone. "No," he told me. "They're more than that. They're real."

CHAPTER 8

Devils

My dear brothers, never forget, when you hear the progress of enlightenment vaunted, that the devil's best trick is to persuade you that he doesn't exist!

—CHARLES BAUDELAIRE

IF YOU ARE interested in angels—and particularly, if you are interested in really believing in angels in this age when it is so hard to do so—then you have to be interested in demons. You don't have to like them, but there is not a writer who has spoken seriously about angels without speaking seriously about demons as well. The list of important figures who took demons seriously goes back to Jesus, who spoke to them all the time, through Saint Paul, to Saint Augustine, to Thomas Aquinas, to Dante, Shakespeare . . . and so on.

Interest in demons stretches the other way as well, of course, as far back into history as we are able to see. Christianity sees demons as fallen angels, and if we look at primordial cultures around the world we see this idea prefigured constantly. The Fall is a universal theme, appearing in mythologies everywhere—a fact that disturbed some Christians when anthropologists discovered it in the nineteenth century, but which writers like C. S. Lewis took easily in stride. For to be a Christian does not demand denying or turning one's eyes from the mythological prefigurings of the Christian story found all over the world. As Lewis—as believing a Christian as one could ask for—reasoned: Why should there not be such prefigurings? If the story of Jesus is the defining story of humankind, why would one not see anticipations and echoes of it everywhere in human history?

> *There is not a writer who has spoken seriously about angels without speaking seriously about demons as well.*

The same goes for the story of Satan, the adversary who tempted Eve into a domain of knowledge that shattered the privileged position that she and Adam, the primordial humans, enjoyed before his meddling. This story appears everywhere as well, from the stories of Native Americans to the ancient Greeks. The story is universal because the event it describes is universal: the human entrance into a knowledge of the moral dimension of the cosmos.

It continues to show up today as well, not in the form of myths, but in real life.

I first came across Joe Fisher's name while doing the research for a book of mine called *The Modern Book of the Dead*. Fisher had written some well-regarded books on spiritual topics. But far and away his most interesting book to me was one called *Hungry Ghosts* (later republished under the title *The Siren Call of Hungry Ghosts*). In this book, Fisher relates how, during the course of writing a book with Dr. Joel Whitton, a psychologist, he'd heard of a "channeling circle" that took place weekly in an apartment not too far from him in Toronto. Fisher joined the group and began to take regular part in it. During the sessions a woman he calls Aviva Neumann (not her real name) fell into a trance and spoke on behalf of a half dozen spiritual beings. These beings, decidedly bossy in nature, soon had Fisher completely in their thrall, and he began to fall prey to the delusion that he was on the verge of what he saw as the single greatest discovery in history: proof (there's that word again) that the soul survives death. Fisher was by all accounts a nice guy—pleasant, well-intentioned, and hardworking, with a wide set of interests and a serious dedication to the craft of journalism. But he was also possessed by certain weaknesses of character—gaps in his personality that the entities who appear to have been working through Aviva quickly identified and took advantage of. Reading his story, it is remarkable to see how closely the beings he came into contact with adhere to the list of behaviors attributed to demons by Jesus, Saint Paul, and such early Christian writers as Gregory of Nyssa and Basil of Caesarea.

One of Fisher's shortcomings was an inability to establish a really solid romantic relationship. Though he had had his share of girlfriends, Fisher had never really been able to connect and remain with a partner for any length of time. Fisher's parents were British, and he admired the bond his parents (his father was a minister) had formed. But he had never succeeded in forming such a bond himself, and he was, at the time he joined the channeling circle, doubtful that he ever would.

One of the things I immediately liked about *The Siren Call of Hungry Ghosts* was the candor with which Fisher laid forth his story. His tone was patently sincere and honest, and it made it easy to continue to believe him as his book became ever more bizarre, outlandish, and genuinely disturbing. Fisher, during the writing of the book, actually loses his mind, and, in a very frightening way, we follow right along with him as he does.

When it came to Fisher's difficulties in securing a lasting romantic bond, the spirits were happy to step in. They supplied Fisher with the solution to his troubles in the form of a beautiful young Greek girl named Filipa, with whom he had apparently shared a past life several centuries before on the coast of Greece.

At first, Filipa didn't speak directly to Fisher. He was simply told of her existence by the other spirits and encouraged to meditate on her every day, trying to bring her being into his. Eventually, however, Filipa's voice, distinctly different from all the other channeled voices, came "through" Aviva Neumann, and Fisher learned directly from Filipa further details of their intense but ill-fated romance in the Greece of several hundred years ago. Fisher found himself counting the minutes each week until it was time for them to meet again.

Page by page, Fisher loses ever further touch with reality and with the people in his life, and it is clear—to the reader at least—that this is just what the spirits want. His friends advise him to discontinue the experiment. His mother, on a phone call from England, says that she believes him when he says the beings he is talking to are real. But she says she also believes that they are demons, and she doesn't like it one bit.

Fisher's real-life girlfriend, meanwhile, at first tolerant of his attendance at the weekly séances, eventually grows tired of sharing Joe with his new spiritual girlfriend. After all, it is easy enough to see that he finds Filipa considerably more interesting than the mere flesh-and-blood being she is. Fisher and his girlfriend break up, and he has full freedom to pursue his relationship with Filipa.

As Fisher's infatuation with Filipa grows, so does his sense of mission. He feels—and hears—Filipa inside him, knowing she is there from a particular buzzing sound he gets in his ears. He develops an all but messianic urge to demonstrate proof to the world that death is an illusion. At lunch with a trusted friend who has published some of his articles, he is asked directly why he continues with an experiment that is clearly having negative effects on him. Fisher answers honestly: Because the world as it is just doesn't make sense.

> *That demons mix truth with lies was a fact well known to Jesus and Paul as well. Demons have power. If they didn't, the New Testament authors wouldn't have bothered talking about them as much as they do.*

Yet another remarkable aspect of the book to me was how much, at least initially, the information given by the spirits lined up with checkable facts (That demons mix truth with lies was a fact well known to Jesus and Paul as well. Demons have power. If they didn't, the New Testament authors wouldn't have bothered talking about them as much as they do). One spirit in particular supplied Fisher with details of the last weeks of his former life on earth when he was a British aviator during World War II. Fisher travels to England to check out some of the more obscure details this spirit gives him, and they line up. Stunningly, inexplicably, the spirits are on the mark again and again. Fisher is on the verge of generating a revolution in our understanding of the physical and spiritual worlds that will literally change the course of history. Or so he thinks.

Then, slowly but surely, things begin to slip. With a surprise equal to that which he experienced when he came across all the details the spirits got right, he now discovers that they are starting to get a lot of stuff wrong. Demoralized and infuriated, Fisher confronts the spirits. How do they explain their errors in fact that he has uncovered?

As spirits will, they dissemble. They do their best to slide around the issue, and when Fisher persists, they get angry. Fisher determines the great test of whether the spirits are real or not will come with a trip to Greece—specifically to the area where he and Filipa were supposed to have played out the drama of their doomed romantic relationship. Laboriously, Fisher locates and travels to the exact area the spirits have described, only to discover yet another long and devastating series of discrepancies. The spirits, it seems, are full of baloney.

And yet, even after the reader has long lost patience with Fisher, a question lingers about these patently untrustworthy beings that are slowly but surely driving him mad: Who are they? For halfway through the book, one can't help but get the feeling that Fisher really *is* talking to someone, or something, other than the frail and not overwhelmingly interesting woman that all these voices are emanating from. The words that Fisher's mother had spoken on the phone return again and again to the reader's mind: "You're talking to demons. And I don't like the sound of it one bit."

At long last, Fisher disengages from the spirits and stops going to the weekly meetings. He publishes the first edition of *Hungry Ghosts*, issuing dire warnings to anyone else who might, like he was, be tempted into such explorations. His descriptions of the spirits who have deceived him so are far beyond unflattering. They are damning.

Hungry Ghosts came out originally in 1990 and several years later was republished, this time in the edition and under the title that I read: *The Siren Call of Hungry Ghosts*. This edition contains an epilogue explaining what Fisher has been up to since the original edition came out. Most fascinatingly, he describes suffering an infection of the navel, an extremely rare and extremely painful condition usually suffered only by newly born children.

The navel, as Fisher notes in his description of his ordeal, is a very symbolic part of the body. It is our center and represents our connection to the spiritual world that brought us forth. In seeking to infect him there, it is almost as if the spirits were doing more than simply antagonizing him. They were trying to remove his very center, to knock him from his bearings and send him once and for all into the miasmal outer darkness where they dwell. (In this they are doing exactly the opposite of what guardian angels are said to do: keep one centered on the beam of one's essential self, just as the beings behind Lindbergh on his journey across the Atlantic were set on helping him stay on course.)

The reissue of the book came out on May 8, 2001. Fisher killed himself, jumping from a cliff near his isolated cabin outside Toronto, the next day, May 9.

Why tell this sad and troubling story in a book that is supposed to be about angels? The answer is simple. Stories like Fisher's can be very helpful. Why? Because they get under our skin. They line up with astonishing precision with what scripture tells us of demons, but we do not need to squint across centuries to see them. These occurrences happen right here, right now, and in that closeness to us there is a great benefit: they can convince people otherwise uninterested in the possibility that demons, fallen angels, and suchlike things might actually be real. I can't claim to understand exactly whom or what Fisher was talking to, but his book was strong enough to convince me he was talking to *something*. The possibility that these beings were not only real but malevolent is also valuable, for if we are able to acknowledge that evil genuinely exists, that it is a real force in the world, then it becomes a lot easier to acknowledge that good exists as well. In other words: if evil is real, then so (most likely) is good.

And if good and evil are real and not empty abstractions in a world without meaning (the world materialism asserts we live in) then paradoxically enough, that is good news. For if there is one thing that, if true, is worse than the fact that evil exists in our world, it is the possibility that evil *doesn't* exist. The polarities of Good and Evil, if they are living spiritual realities and not just words, are all the evidence we need to realize that we live in a world that started somewhere, that is going somewhere, that is saturated at every point with meaning, and in which we play an active, and perhaps crucial, part. We are given back our true dignity as spiritual beings living momentarily in a physical world that is itself but a small part of a much, much larger spiritual world.

If you go out walking, and you find yourself in a murky swamp that leaves your shoes soaked through when you get home, the point to focus on is not the mud, but the water. In a world where there are murky swamps, there must also be lakes, and rivers, and seas. If there is a true and real world of Evil with a capital *E*, then there is a true and real world of Good with a capital *G*.

Where there are demons, there are angels. Where there is a hell, there is a heaven. Where there are inexplicable events and actions, there is a larger, more-than-physical world where these events and actions have come from, and within which they can, perhaps, be found to have meaning. And—though of course this last bit asks for faith, not philosophy—there is a God who sees and cares about it all.

On December 14, 2012, I drove up to Great Barrington, Massachusetts, to visit a friend of mine named Chris Bamford. Along with my friend Gene Gollogly, Chris is the publisher of Steiner-Books. Rudolf Steiner was an Austrian philosopher of the late nineteenth and early twentieth centuries, the author of many books, and the creator of biodynamic farming and the Waldorf school system. Steiner was a genius, but a controversial and often difficult one to understand. He was also a Christian and a student of the invisible world, but his works are extremely challenging, and it has been chiefly through Chris's writings on Steiner that I have come to understand his vision of life at least a little. Chris is one of the very few people I know who I suspect really does walk around without that glass helmet on.

I visit Chris at least once a year, because there is never a time when I do that I don't learn something that I remember later—that sticks with me. On this visit, it was a fairly simple statement on Chris's part that brought me up short.

"The thing I've been thinking about recently," said Chris, "is that it's all . . . right here."

He gestured around to the sidewalk we were on, with its health-food shops and gift stores. "The angelic hierarchies are all right here, right now. We are in the middle of them, but we don't see them."

As it happened, the day of that visit to Chris was also the day of the Sandy Hook school shooting. Driving up to Great Barrington from Nyack, New York, where I live, I passed close by Newtown, Connecticut, and was little more than half an hour away from it when I heard the first reports of the event on the radio. Now, several years later, when I open my computer and see yet another report of another shooting at a school or a mall or wherever, I think of a picture I saw of Adam Lanza's room—of how the windows were taped off so that not a bit of light could get in. Lonely and cut-off as that young man was, I'm quite sure that sealed-off room of his was anything but empty.

So the message of evil entities is essentially the same as the message of the angels: the world is bigger than we think it is, and we are more than we think we are. Our fates are larger than our earthly ones, and that is only underlined when an individual's earthly fate is especially short and tragic. That was the message hidden in the Boren horror—the message that Tyler finally gleaned from it, thanks to the work of those two beings at his legs, who felt his pity and sadness and sought to console him.

CHAPTER 9

Where Do We Go?

"All of us have monarchs and sages for kinsmen; nay, angels and archangels for cousins; since in antediluvian days, the sons of God did verily wed with our mothers, the irresistible daughters of Eve. Thus all generations are blended: and heaven and earth of one kin: the hierarchies of seraphs in the uttermost skies; the thrones and principalities in the zodiac; the shades that roam throughout space; the nations and families, flocks and folds of the earth; one and all, brothers in essence—oh, be we then brothers indeed! All things form but one whole."

—HERMAN MELVILLE, *MARDI*

SOMETIMES TYLER AND the other cops talked about it, about what was happening to the world, and America, and what was missing now that hadn't been missing before. And if a word came up regularly to describe what was missing now, what was fading away more and more with each year in the country, it was this: *community*. It used to be built around the churches, the churches with their leaders who, Tyler now knew, were sometimes flawed in terrible ways. Tyler knew most church leaders weren't like that, and he certainly knew that most Mormon leaders weren't like that. He respected the religion he'd grown up in. But the fact that it could happen at all . . . that there could even *be* people like that, and that they could get away with it, at least sometimes, signified to him that the fabric was wearing thin, that it was now more susceptible to rips and tears. And that just ate him up.

Tyler and I are twenty-three years apart, and among the many generation gap items that separate us is music. But one day I couldn't resist referencing a song from the years when I was his age. "You know that Guns n' Roses song 'Sweet Child o' Mine'?" I once asked him.

"Oh sure," he said. "Everyone knows that song."

"Well, you know that part at the end where Axl just keeps asking, 'Where do we go now?' I always kind of thought Axl had America's number pretty well there. You know, like— where *do* we go now?"

"Yeah," said Tyler. "That's the problem for sure. Where do we go? I ask that pretty much every day."

Like a lot of Mormon communities, Spanish Fork isn't unwelcoming to other churches, other faiths. Tyler's mom, Pam, told me about a group of Hare Krishnas who were, if not a prominent, certainly a highly noticeable presence in the area.

"Hare *Krishnas*?" I said, incredulous. (I have to admit I've long held a grudge against the Hare Krishnas for pushing a copy of the Bhagavad Gita on me in an airport back in the early seventies when I was too young to realize I was being swindled.) "So what are they like?"

"Oh," said Pam, "they couldn't be nicer. They have a food co-op at the end of Main Street, and a wonderful float on Fiesta Day."

"Fiesta Day?"

"Yes, it celebrates the day the Mormon Church was founded here."

Tyler, it seemed to me, with his upbringing in such a forgiving town, with his natural faith in life and his unforced outrage at what the world had become, was a real-life embodiment of a type of character who appears often in fictional stories: the Good-Hearted Soul or Noble Innocent. This character tends to have a rocky time of it, for he starts out believing that the world is a good and pure place but learns by hard experience that it is not quite as good as he had thought, that there is injustice and downright evil mixed in with it as well. That it's also not a place where good always triumphs and evil is always brought to justice. It is, instead, a place where you get a dog, name him Lucky, and a jerk down the street runs him over. A place where a man, crazy from grief or anger or both, can throw his own son around his house, then place him carefully in bed and go down to the basement and shoot himself. A place where good exists, to be sure, but where evil exists as well, and all too often seems to be far more prevalent and powerful.

Yet in literature at least, if this hapless yet noble character perseveres, he often arrives at a moment of understanding. This moment can be big and dramatic, or so small that the reader might almost miss it when it happens. This is the moment when, for the troubled young hero of the story, the jar breaks. The moment when he (or, of course, she) sees that though the world is indeed a terrible place, there is far more going on in it than first meets the eye. For behind it there lies another world: one where Good and Evil are both extremely real, but where Good is triumphant in exactly the way it so often fails to be in the ordinary world.

Throughout our interviews, I'd pushed Tyler to tell me about his life in as honest and forthcoming a manner as possible, and he'd made a truly heroic effort to comply. He had, I was more than aware, not enjoyed telling me how Jenny's face had looked when he and the other policemen had succeeded in turning over her car. He had not enjoyed telling me about the boy thrown around the house by his father, or the way the Boren clan had looked, lined up in bed. These were horrors, all of them, and I knew, as I asked Tyler for one detail after another, that a part of him was wondering what my purpose could possibly be in asking him about them. Toward the end of our interviews, then, it was no surprise that he made a point of telling me how he was different now—how what happened at the Spanish Fork Bridge had tripped some wire in him that had allowed him to move from despair, to a new state of mind: one he was still in the process of understanding.

Some of the details he gave me in these final interviews were pretty amusing. In one, he told me how he'd pretty much stopped having a drink of Crown Royal when he got home now—that he didn't need to numb himself after work so much, even if it had been a really bad day.

"Whiskey?" I said. "I thought you said you drank beer!"

"Yeah," Tyler said guiltily. "That was the one thing I told

you that wasn't true. I thought if you knew it was whiskey it would make me look like a really bad guy."

Tyler told me about how two or three times a week, he now likes to hike up to the big concrete "Y" that sits over Brigham Young University, and how he sits in it and looks down at the whole stretch of the Pioneer Valley and all the towns in it, and out to Utah Lake, and, beyond that, to the horizon. "The world's still going to hell," Tyler told me. "But it's different now, it really is. This probably sounds corny, but it seems to me that maybe God puts us down here to test us. That this is all some big way of allowing us to find out who we really are."

As someone who had spent a fair amount of time reading about myths, legends, and the way the details of ordinary human lives often line up strangely with the plots of those myths and legends, I had long since given up on worrying where Tyler's thoughts and experiences would lead him next. I was, at this point, simply along for the ride, so I just asked him if he had anything else he might like to add to the story of what happened at the Spanish Fork Bridge, and the days and weeks after, and how it had changed him.

"Well," said Tyler, hesitation in his voice, "there is one particular thing, yeah."

"What was it?"

"Well," Tyler said, "it's kind of negative."

"You leave that to me to worry about," I said. "Just tell me the story."

"It was back in July," Tyler said. "When we were about half-way along with all this. It was around three in the afternoon. I was in my squad car, and a call came out that there were reports of a guy acting erratically, walking around and just saying crazy stuff. One report said he had a gun. The last report put him near a Mormon church on the corner of East and Center Streets. I headed over there, and so did another cop, a friend of mine, in another squad car.

"I get to the church and there's a big field next to it. I decide to pull up and see if I can see anyone out in the field. I'm scanning around, about to get out of my car, when suddenly four shots go off right behind me."

"What did you think it was?" I asked.

"I *knew* what it was," Tyler told me. "I knew exactly what it was. My buddy had pulled into the lot behind the church, and obviously he'd run right up on the guy. One of the two had been shot. I got out of the car and ran around to the back of the church. I didn't know what I was running into, just no idea."

Tyler turned the corner and froze. There before him in the lot behind the church was the man the reports had come in about, lying on his back. The reports that he'd had a gun were correct. It was in his hand. Facing him was Tyler's buddy.

"So your friend shot him."

"He had to," Tyler said. "My buddy said, 'He raised his gun on me.' He said it in a daze. When someone raises a gun on you, you have to fire first. You just have to do it, instantly. It's trained into us. Otherwise you're dead. I ran over and did CPR with the breath bag and tried to bring the guy around. But there was nothing. He was dead."

"What did you do next?"

"I got up and walked over to my buddy. He was just standing there, starting to tear up. I mean here's this guy, he's standing there with a handgun in this year of all years, where everyone thinks if you wear a cop's uniform you're a killer. And I can see he's just a total mess. He's taken a guy's life. This cop, my friend—he's one of the good guys, and he's shattered by what's happened. Not because he thinks he's made a mistake, but because he understands the implications, the enormity, of taking another person's life. It's like he's stepped out of the human rule book and into God's. In a situation like this, even if you know it was the right thing to do, in that it was the only option open to you, all the same, you suddenly see how big the universe is, and that maybe there's other laws, and who's to say if you haven't just broken one, and what it really means?"

"So what did you do?"

Tyler paused a moment. "I just hugged him and said, 'You did the right thing.'"

From the way he told me this, I knew that Tyler must have done so without a moment's hesitation. Almost as if a little voice had told him so.

—⦾—

CHAPTER 10

Proof?

Fifteen years ago I was on a bus traveling through the night
between Amherst, Massachusetts and Syracuse, New York.
Toward the beginning of the trip a group of people boarded,
including a young woman who sat a couple of seats behind
me. I had just completed an intense weekend of meditation and
spiritual exercises. After a while the young woman moved up
to the empty seat next to me. "Hello," she said. She then told
me many things about myself. I felt comfortably but strangely
transparent. It seemed as though I were in a field of magic, and
the laws of nature had been interrupted. I had a strong desire
to hear more and talk and get to know this woman as a person,
but just then the bus arrived in the small town of Lenox, and
she walked to the front and stepped down into the darkness.

—PSYCHOLOGIST THOMAS MOORE

EVIDENCE OF THE reality of the spiritual world is not in
short supply. We are drowning in it. But what we do with this
evidence is up to each of us. Every spiritual experience, every

encounter with a being beyond the boundary of the merely physical, whether it happens to us or whether we hear about it from
someone else, is like a football, thrown high and long, straight at
us. We can do two things with this football. We can use every bit
of our ability to catch and run with it, or we can let it drop to the
ground. Grasping the proof of all such events demands effort
on our part. If we are not willing to expend that effort, no bit of
evidence, no matter how strong, will convince us.

*Evidence of the reality of the spiritual world is
not in short supply. We are drowning in it.*

All "proof," including the most rigorous scientific kind,
demands effort on our part to apprehend, and that effort is *always* somehow creative in nature. If we fail to make that effort,
we will not grasp *any* of the truths the world offers us. What it
comes down to in the end is whether we are willing to accept
certain truths that go contrary to beliefs we already have. That
is precisely the position that people who refuse to look at all evidence of the miraculous today are in. They don't buy it, because
they are not open for a second to have it sold to them. So in the
end, nothing will do it. If we don't want to be convinced, we
don't have to be.

So how can you prove angels exist? One absolutely correct
answer is to say, simply, that you can't. You can't prove angels
exist in the way that you can prove that salt is made of sodium
chloride, or that two objects of different weight fall at the same

speed in a vacuum. You cannot prove that angels, or anything spiritual, exists by exerting human power on it, because the spiritual is immune to human power.

> *You can't prove angels exist in the way that you can prove that salt is made of sodium chloride, or that two objects of different weight fall at the same speed in a vacuum.*

I experienced that fact firsthand while working with Eben Alexander on his book, *Proof of Heaven*. The title of that book, come up with at the last minute, was mine, and at first Eben balked at it a bit. Proof? Wasn't that a little strong? "Suppose," Eben said, "we called it *My Proof of Heaven*?"

But once the word *proof* was out, it was hard for anyone to get it back in the bag. That word ended up propelling Eben, when the book came out, into a stratosphere of seemingly never-ending controversy, one that I, from my spot on the ground, watched with ever-increasing wonder and fascination. After that, when reading a book about philosophy or religion, I became sensitive to when and where the word *proof* showed up. I soon noticed that one of the first things many writers on the reality of the spiritual dimension said was that spiritual reality in fact could not be "proved."

But there is a different kind of proof than the one so many of the skeptics who complained about *Proof of Heaven* talked about. A proof just as real, just as solid, but different in focus. Many, many people have seen angels. Likewise, many, many people have heard angels speaking in their ear, giving them advice at just the right moment. Some have felt the touch of their hand upon their shoulder.

Meanwhile, no one on earth, not a single person, has ever once seen, much less handled and examined, an electron, or a proton, or a quark, or gravity, or dozens of other modern discoveries that we have been trained to think of in naively concrete terms. That's not to say that they *aren't* realities, of course. But it *is* to say that it's not fair, and not correct, to tell someone who has seen an angel that such things are not realities—that they don't exist because they don't fit in with the picture of the universe that has been hammered into us by our culture since birth. If you are positive that angels don't exist, then you've got your helmet securely on, and you think you see the world with full and total clarity. And, in fact, you do. But you're seeing only half of it.

Angels, the most intense manifestation of the divine world that we can see (for as God explained to Moses, if we saw him we would die), have appeared not only to a great number of individuals, but also to a great number of groups of people as well. Cokeville is a fantastically vivid example of this phenomenon, but it is far from the only one, and if you want to read about more, open Jovanovic's book, or Mark Booth's *The Sacred History*, each of which contains dozens. Were all the people who saw these things crazy or deluded? Maybe. But we live now in a world where deciding who is crazy or deluded is not nearly as easy as it was, say, 150 years ago, when it was generally thought that science was on the brink of explaining everything in the universe.

The last-minute reversal of our confident plan to know everything about the universe came early in the twentieth century, with the appearance of modern physics. Just as we were on the verge of living in a world made up solely of atoms—tiny little objects, each one hard as a rock and easy to measure and predict—those atoms suddenly vanished into thin air. Solid matter, physicists discovered, wasn't solid at all. That solidity was just an illusion created by us when we gazed out at the material world. We perceive our world as solid because our eyes and brains are wired to do so. In fact, the material world isn't made of "material" at all, but an invisible force called energy. What is energy made of? No one, as yet, has an answer. So it was that, just a short century ago, the measurable, knowable world that science was getting so comfortable with measuring, understanding, and controlling, vanished with an abrupt *poof.*

This is fascinating, but it is also terrifying. For it turns out that though those who believed only in the material world thought they were being wonderfully brave in comparison to the poor ignorant cowards who pretended there was a God in order to get through the day, in fact just the opposite was the case.

It turned out that believing in God was much, much scarier than just believing in material reality. Why? Because if there are only atoms, and consciousness is just a wispy sort of nothing that appears for a moment and then is gone, and nothing of us survives the death of the material body and the shutting down of the material brain, we have an escape hatch from the world. It's called death. To get away from the horror of the world, all we have to do is die.

But if the spiritual world exists? That is infinitely scarier. For that means, basically, *there is no getting out of this.*

So ever since materialism lost its footing about a hundred years ago (though of course many materialists continue to think its footing remains as secure as ever), we have been living in a world without a floor—a world without any certainties, in which neither science nor religion can save us from that uncertainty.

Living in a world like this produces panic. As the writer Philip Roth has suggested, if each of us were even remotely in touch with how terrified we actually are about living in such a meaningless and valueless and pain-filled universe, we would instantly go insane. Is that exaggerating? Not in the least. It is really the one fact everyone, from Baptists to Buddhists to the most hardheaded of materialists, can agree on.

Today, perhaps more than ever before in history, we live in a world of uncertainty. From the economy to the climate to the terrible things members of different faiths are doing to one another, few times—and many would say no time ever—have been quite as unsettling as this one.

In this world without certainties, the idea—and perhaps the stunning reality—of angels might have something important to teach us. Something that might help us now more than it has ever helped before. Why? Because angels are the most singularly fantastic and powerful answer to the horror of the world there is. Angels are not the highest things in the world. (God, and if you are a Christian, God and Jesus, are higher than the angels. Just as, indeed, we are—potentially—which is why Satan is said to have gotten so mad at God for creating us. Again and again in the Bible and among the church fathers, it is stressed that though the angels are superior to us in many ways, ultimately it is we humans who are the truly singular beings of God's creation. What is so wonderful about this idea is the message of hope it gives us. We are, this line of thinking would argue, beings with a true future: beings who are *on the way* somewhere. This world we see is not all there is, so this linear, temporal life we are all leading is not all there is to our story. There is more—much more—to come.) But traditionally, and in practice, angels are the highest beings that appear to us down here. And it is that moment of experience, that moment when an angel appears, that is so extraordinarily valuable, for it answers instantly the nightmare of existence. In a flash, the world we thought we were stuck in is broken—shattered like glass.

If a materialist (someone who believes the world is composed of protons, neutrons, electrons, and the subatomic particles that in turn make them up, and nothing else) tells you the contrary, that there is no evidence whatsoever for the existence of purely spiritual beings that show up at unpredictable times and then vanish, you can be pretty sure that he or she hasn't spent much, or any, time with the vast amount of serious and convincing literature on the subject: literature written not by crystal-gazing tarot readers at mini-malls (not that I have anything against crystal-gazing tarot readers), but people like Gertude Rachel Levy, an accomplished archaeologist and a major figure in British archaeology throughout the middle years of the twentieth century.

Levy, as she revealed in her 1964 book *The Phoenix' Nest*, was throughout her adult life in near constant contact with a being that acted as her guide on earth—her spiritual counselor, in essence. Or to use a more common term, he was her guardian angel.

The literature on immaterial tutelary beings—spirits who

communicate regularly with certain men and women and guide them in their decisions and actions in life—is very large, and a lot of it is very hard to discount, other than by simply waving it away without looking at it. This last strategy is very popular, however, and so it is that books like Levy's—a book that purely on the strength of its author's academic credentials and her intellectual achievements in life should have been qualified for serious consideration when it came out—are instead ignored and quickly forgotten. Levy, not surprisingly, expected as much and wrote in the book itself that she wrote it not to garner attention or create a stir, but because she felt that her experiences of the other world had so convinced her of the reality of that dimension and the beings within it that it deserved to be reported about no matter what the personal consequences to her might be. All the same, our dominant intellectual culture still insists on treating all spiritual phenomena somatically—that is, as a function of the body, and more specifically, the brain—even though ordinary people go about having experiences that defy this kind of explanation every day. A stranger shows up at an auto accident, provides a crucial piece of assistance, and vanishes without anyone getting his or her name. People find themselves "guided" through life by inner voices that speak up just when something potentially dangerous is about to happen. An object appears at a certain time and place, just when a certain person needed it to, with no explanation for how it did so.

Silliness? Maybe. But it is a remarkably resilient variety of silliness: one that goes on all the time, without anyone in the materialist community being able to explain even the smallest part of it away. But of course, these things don't always happen when we want them to. They don't appear on demand. A young child playing on a beach gets swept out to sea. No rescuing hand comes from out of nowhere to pull her to shore. She drowns. If there is an invisible world crowded with invisible beings just dying to help us, the materialist community reasonably argues, they certainly seem to miss a lot of opportunities to do so.

To say the spiritual exists, that it is (at least in large part) a good place, and that it desires our well-being does not mean that we understand how that world works, why it manifests when it does, and why it so much more frequently doesn't manifest at all, just when we might most have liked it to.

The piece of literature that addresses this fact most directly is, of course, the book of Job. In that story, God, goaded on by Satan (who in that book is less a figure of evil than a kind of sideman throwing God conundrums to deal with), is given all sorts of opportunities to help an individual who clearly deserves it. Instead, everything is taken from him. The "moral" of the book of Job is generally agreed to be that part of having religious faith—a big part—is accepting that the events of this world don't turn out exactly as we'd like them to. Drowning children aren't always saved, and water glasses don't go smashing against the wall, even at moments when if they did, such an event would provide a wonderful opportunity to convince many people who don't believe in God or the invisible world in general to change their minds.

But then again, sometimes events do work that way. And they have done so many, many more times than once. Why here and not there? Why to this person but not that one? That answer is the same now as it was when the book of Job was written: God's ways are not our ways. We don't know.

To prove a thing or creature or phenomenon exists, one does not need to keep on proving it exists again and again. One needs, in fact, only to demonstrate convincingly that it happened once.

But here's the important thing: when it comes to establishing the actual existence of a spiritual world, that doesn't matter. As the nineteenth-century American philosopher and creator of the discipline of psychology William James pointed out more than a century ago, to prove a thing or creature or phenomenon exists, one does not need to keep on proving it exists again and again. One needs, in fact, only to demonstrate convincingly that it happened once.

Science—specifically, the experimental method on which science is built—argues that for something to be scientifically true, it must be shown to exist in the right-in-front-of-us physical world whenever we want it to and as many times as we want it to. We can make sodium chloride by mixing hydrochloric acid and sodium hydroxide all day and all night, and the results will always be the same. That's the scientific method, and it's how we determine if a phenomenon is real or not.

Yet at the same time, there are many experiments in physics at the quantum level that are devilishly hard to make happen again and again. In recent years, certain subatomic reactions are becoming harder and harder to reproduce, even though a few decades ago they were (comparatively) easy to bring about. How on earth are we to explain this? As yet, no one can.

The primary argument of many of the greatest religious texts, both ancient and modern, is that the "rules" of the spiritual world cannot be explained from the standpoint of this world—the immediate, plain-as-nails physical one right in front of us. Just as angels are actual, personal beings but not *human* beings, so the spiritual world has rules and regulations, but they are not the rules and regulations of our world. Its parameters of explanation are much larger, and we flatter ourselves when we imagine that we have anything more than the remotest grasp of what they are. This seems, at least to me, an argument that we should listen to.

CHAPTER 11

What It All Means

Perhaps all the dragons of our lives are princesses who are only waiting to see us once beautiful and brave.

—RAINER MARIA RILKE

W HEN YOU WRITE a book, you enter into the subject matter. You get infected by it. Or at least, you had better hope you get infected by it, because a writer who isn't hit by his subject matter doesn't have any business writing to begin with.

For me, that moment when I was truly hit by what I had been writing about came when Tyler mentioned an email he'd received a few weeks before but which he hadn't noticed because it had gone to his spam folder. "It's from Jenny's sister," he said.

"Her sister?"

All through the writing of this book, I'd kept my focus entirely on Tyler and his experiences. Because Tyler was so authentic and because his story was so compelling, I'd felt it allowed me to overcome my trepidation about going any deeper into Jenny's life. If I just stuck with what happened at the bridge, I told myself, I didn't have to worry about compromising Jenny, about dishonoring the life, and the death, of someone I'd never even met by writing about it.

With a sentence, Tyler had just turned that plan upside down. "What did the email say? Did you call her?"

"No," Tyler said. "The email was nice: it just said how she'd read there was a book being done about the crash, and she was just curious."

"Give me the number," I said.

Tyler dug up the number, we hung up, and I dialed it. A pleasant voice answered, and, my heart beating a little hard, I told her who I was and what I'd been doing.

I ended up reading Jill, Jenny's sister, the chapter about her death on the Spanish Fork Bridge. As I did so, I had exactly the feeling that Tyler had told me about in the story of what had happened to his officer friend behind the church: the feeling that I had strayed out of the ordinary rule book of life and into another kind of rule book. One written not by humans, but by an authority larger than that. After I'd finished reading, we hung up, and Jill emailed Tyler. As Tyler told me the next day, her message was short and to the point. "She told me," Tyler said, "'I'm so sorry you had to see my baby sister like that.'"

Through Jill, I got to know the young woman whose death I had been writing about with such care but whose life I had somehow not found the strength to face. And slowly, thanks to her friendliness to a writer who out of the blue had forced her to see the direct horror of her sister's death, my misgivings, my feelings of guilt, eased up. Jill told me that ever since their mom had died tragically in a fire six years ago, Jenny had been obsessed with what had happened to her mom and with where she was now.

"She wouldn't let it go," Jill told me. "She thought about it all the time. It was like she just couldn't get reconciled with her mom's death. With the fact that something like that could happen in a world which, generally, she loved so much."

"Do you think," I asked Jill, "that Jenny might have intentionally taken a kind of hard right turn off the road of her life?"

"Well, you know," she told me, "it's weird. Because when I finally got the nerve to go and look at that intersection where it happened, I just couldn't believe it. I couldn't believe how narrow the place was where she went through."

"Tyler," I said, "told me that he could practice all day and still not get his car to do what hers had. So . . . what does that mean? Do you think she did it on purpose?"

Jill told me she didn't. She told me she didn't understand it, she knew she never *would* understand it, but she knew that Jenny loved life, and her daughter, too much to ever have done that on purpose.

Jill sent me a lot of photos of Jenny, and as the stepfather of three girls I was haunted by how completely familiar the pictures looked. In most of them Jenny had her left arm raised toward the camera in the manner that indicates the photo is a selfie, and I recognized every expression, every attitude. There were the posed, pouty, sultry ones; the goofy ones; and the just plain regular ones, in which I could see who Jenny was more clearly than through all the others: a girl with a beautiful smile, a little too much eye makeup, and a big heart.

One of the things that intrigued me most was some writing on her arm. When I saw it in one photo, I thought maybe it was just temporary. But when it kept showing up, I realized it was a tattoo. But I couldn't make out the words. What did they say?

I asked in an email, and Jill responded. "Oh gosh . . . the writing on my sister's arm. I love it and she loooooved that tattoo. It's about our mom. When I was preparing the program for our mom's funeral I made a little handout with her photo. I will send you a pic. It's from a Sarah McLachlan song and it says, 'You gave me everything you had, oh you gave me light . . . and I will remember you.'

"When I was at the mortician's examining Jenny's body to decide if it would be appropriate to have an open-casket viewing I stared at her tattoo for a long time, morbidly wishing I could somehow take her arm with me. When I spoke at Jenny's funeral I talked about her tattoo . . . and closed with those words . . . barely not choking, of course."

So the words on Jenny's arm were about loss, and about the love that overcomes loss. They were about the refusal to give up hope, the refusal, when a loved one dies, to accept that he or she is completely gone. The dogged, determined faith that those we love are not, in fact, *ever* truly gone. That they are simply in a place where we can no longer see them as we did when they were alive, but where, in certain rare but all-important moments, we can feel them inside us. Jenny, a young woman I had never met, had exactly the attitude toward death that I'd always had. She refused to take it at face value. She believed—she *knew*—there was something more.

But the email was not finished. "Okay," Jill continued, "the weirdest thing just happened. I got up from this email to take a picture of that funeral handout for you. I was tuning out my girls, who were banging on the piano. Neither of them play . . . they just mess around on it. My daughter was singing and I was ignoring her at first until I realized the words were sounding familiar. I went over and looked at the sheet music she was reading from and it was 'I Will Remember You.' I didn't even know I had piano music for it. Maybe it doesn't sound that weird, but my kids don't know that song or its significance or who Sarah McLachlan is. She dug through old piano books and just happened to turn the page to that song. So weird."

Our helmets can fall away in all kinds of ways. They can fall away in moments of wonder, and they can fall away in moments of terror, or moments of sudden existential culpability. After our helmets fall away, we are in exactly the same world we were a moment before, yet at the same time we are standing in a completely new one. It's the same old horrible world of pain and injustice. Yet it's more than that as well. Much more.

I wrote Jill back my thoughts about that coincidence. I wrote it fast, because I didn't have to think about it at all. "You know, this is the great thing about the world, the thing that really interests me. It is messed up, and horrible beyond all imagining. But, at the same time, and there's no denying this if you really study it, it's just a straight fact—it's SIGNIFICANT. I imagine you know the term *synchronicity*, right? Carl Jung's word for the fact that the world is way, way more tied up with itself than we normally realize. Everything's significant. Everything means something. And yet at the same time, everything is just horribly messed up and full of pain, and it sucks, and on an overcast Sunday afternoon it often seems like the people who say life is meaningless are right. But . . . they're not. And you can't live, you can't make it through life, if you don't come to realize this in a way that you don't just think, but feel in your bones."

Reading the email over before clicking "send," I was taken aback at how totally straightforward and accurate a statement it was. This really was the single fact that I'd spent most of my life thinking about. And here, at the end of this book, was that exact truth being handed to me by the sister of a girl I'd never known, whose life I had no business writing about, but who had somehow, some way, broadened my view of things and increased my own hope. The helmet I wear on my own head had been loosened just a little more.

As we neared the end of the writing process, I decided to go back to the beginning—to get a few more details about the incident at the bridge and its immediate aftermath. We were coming to the end of things, and when you get to the end of something, it's often good to go back to the beginning—to the place you started from—and look at it again to see if it's changed since you first saw it.

Throughout the course of our creating this book, his experience at the bridge—of hearing that voice inside the car—worked on Tyler, worked on him just as the bad experiences had, but in a different way. To his surprise, the memory of what happened that day didn't fade, but stayed at the center of his consciousness at all times, even when other things were going on. It was like a seed planted somewhere within him, and it was a seed that had taken root and was growing. Maybe, it occurred to Tyler, the answer to the riddle of the world was like one of those clues in *Forensic Files*: some detail so small, so seemingly inconsequential that no one had paid any attention to it for the longest time. It was a detail which, when someone finally stopped and did notice it and picked it up and turned it over in the light and examined it, made the whole capsized world turn right side up again.

If the devil, as they say, is in the details, then it seemed like God is to be found there, too. *Forensic Files*, and the other shows like it, had driven home to Tyler, when he was younger, that though the clue is always there, it doesn't just get handed to you. You have to figure out where it is and what it means. That single fiber from the back of some van that was stuck to the jeans of the murdered girl—a fiber that only a specific number of carpets were made of, that were installed in only a specific number of vans, only a specific number of which had been sold in the particular decade in the particular state where the murder had occurred . . . Tyler loved stuff like this. He loved it not for its darkness, but for the way it showed how the world wasn't a totally unfair and terrible place after all, but a place where justice could prevail, where the bad guys could be caught—usually just at that moment when you were absolutely sure they'd escape.

But those programs also showed Tyler that we had some work of our own to do down here. No one ever told the investigators just exactly where the damning evidence of the fibers on the body of the murdered girl were going to be found, or even that any such fibers were there to be found in the first place. But the point was, those investigators had faith that somewhere out there, there was a piece of damning evidence, and that if they looked hard enough and were smart enough, it would show up. And once they found it, that tiny little detail would lead them straight to the bad guy, probably thousands of miles away at that point, his crime forgotten, in some new job, never dreaming he might have made some ridiculous, inconsequential little slipup that would lead to him getting a tap on the shoulder—the tap that told him his ticket was up.

That's what Tyler had learned more than anything else from those *CSI*-type shows. The world didn't make sense on the surface all the time. But scratch that surface, and at depth it made plenty. It had to, after all. There was too much goodness in the world, in people, in animals, in all of creation, for the bad to win out, no matter how much it seemed to be doing so sometimes. Sure, there could be days when the whole world looked upside down. But if you worked hard enough, you could find the clue that turned it right side up again. Things *did* make sense. Justice *was* real. It had to be. Tyler had always aspired to become one of those people who found those little clues—who hunted down and sought out the justice in life, who proved that there was such a thing after all. And in some strange way, Jenny's death and Lily's survival were just such a clue, just such an inspiration to keep going, to keep thinking, to keep open to the possibility that things were stranger, and bigger, and better than they appeared to be.

In the days after what he now was truly convinced was an angel-mediated event at Spanish Fork Bridge, Tyler found himself once again lying awake at night, puzzling about things. Lying awake as he had directly after the Boren shootings, but puzzling now in a different way, in a different key.

"Okay," Tyler told me. "I said: There is a God. I don't understand him, but that doesn't matter. I don't know what happened at that bridge, and I don't know how Lily survived, and I don't know who spoke those words from the car. I'm comfortable calling whoever spoke it an angel, because angels are messengers. And if ever I've been given a message, I was that day, while trying to right that car. What *is* an angel? I know you're supposed to tell folks what they are in this book, but you know, that really is part of what they are: you *can't* tell people what they are, because they're too big, too strange, and too powerful to put a name tag on. But they're real, and if you ask me, that's all the definition you need. So I guess what I know—all I *really* know—is that it happened, it was real, as real as you can get, and that it means something. And the bottom line of what it means is that the world's a big place, and most likely there's a God who's running it, and I gotta trust that he knows what he's doing. When I think about it that way, it just makes me stronger in every cell in my body. I can feel it. And in my experience, when you think about something and it makes you feel strong and good inside, it's usually right."

Tyler also found that each time he told the story of what happened, he was telling it to himself as well. It wasn't as if he had to convince himself the story had happened as it did. He knew it had. He'd heard the voice. But telling it again and again drove it into his head—made it so he couldn't just forget about it, couldn't just pass it off as something crazy and move on. No one knew better than Tyler that with police work, there were certain events, certain images that you couldn't erase from your memory no matter how hard you tried. But the stories you wanted to remember, the ones that were positive and inspiring and made you stronger and better at your job—those stories you had to fight to remember, to keep from having them just slip away. And in spite of the sorrow involved, he wanted this particular story to stay.

Tyler had never been involved in an incident of this media magnitude before, however. As news outfit after news outfit made him go over the details of the day again and again, he found himself getting a little uncomfortable with this new overnight celebrity. After all, he didn't want the story to be about him. But at the same time, he couldn't help noticing how grateful people were to hear the story. It was like they were hungry for it. Not the sad part. Not the terrible fact that a young mother was dead, but the other part, the inexplicable part. Baby Lily's incredible survival. The voice. And the idea, that seemed to come up every time a newscaster told the story, that baby Lily had not been alone down in that horrible black solitude.

Another word popped up a lot with the newscasters. The word sounded a little high and mighty to Tyler's ears, but it wasn't exactly out of place: *miracle.*

The last thing Tyler wanted to do was play any kind of negative role in the legacy of Jennifer Lynn Groesbeck—a woman he'd never met, and whose face, the one time he had seen it, would haunt him for the rest of his life. But maybe by being the spokesman for the miraculous event that had occurred in that car that day, he wasn't doing a disservice to her memory at all, but honoring it. Though Jenny's death was a tragedy, baby Lily's survival was, it seemed, indeed something pretty miraculous, as was the angelic presence that had made her rescue happen.

"I have a friend who works at Payson Hospital where they medevaced Lily up to," Tyler told me. "He knows his stuff. He told me that there was absolutely no way that baby could have made it through that night alive, even with all the stuff that happened in her favor. Yeah, her clothes were dry. Yeah, her mom had dressed her right and strapped her in right. But for a body to be in an upside-down position like that for so many hours, for her to have survived the impact the car made when it hit . . . he gave me a list of detail after detail. They all amounted to one thing: no way. No way that baby should have been alive when we got to her. Then throw in the fact that because we didn't see her there in the backseat, we put her underwater for two minutes—forty-five-degree water. Well, I guess you could put it like this. Fill up your bathtub with water. Dump in a couple of big bags of ice and stir it around. Then get in and sink your head under for two full minutes. Do that, and you get an idea of what that child survived, after the fourteen hours of hanging upside down in a crashed car on a fifty-degree night."

So . . . miracle? Tyler had never given too much thought to what the word really meant, but he figured it boiled down to this: something that can't possibly happen happens anyway. The more he thought about all the details of the story, the more he could see why everyone was so interested, so gratified, to hear him tell it.

❋

"Why Lily and not Jenny?" I asked Tyler during one of our last phone interviews—not because I thought Tyler knew. I knew he didn't. I knew I didn't either. But I wanted to hear what he'd say.

"Well, you know," Tyler said, "the regular answer for that is, 'It's all part of God's plan and we'll know someday,' or something like that."

"Yeah," I said. "That's the standard answer. But what do you think?"

"Well, I guess that's what I think, too. But you know, there's a difference between thinking something and feeling something. I don't know whether I ever thought an answer like that was true before. I might have. But I never felt it. And I guess what that means is that if you haven't felt something, you don't know it."

"That reminds me of something a poet called Kabir said once," I said. "Do you know who Kabir is?"

"Nope," Tyler said.

"Well, he was this fifteenth-century Hindu poet. He said, 'Nothing that hasn't been experienced is true.'"

Tyler thought for a moment.

"Yeah. Yeah, that's it," he said. "I *do* know. I know it because I feel it. In the end, the good feelings I got from the Boren case, from Jenny and Lily, outweighed the bad feelings I got. What happened at the river made me go back to what I'd experienced in the Boren bedroom, what I'd experienced a million times in all kinds of different ways.

"Evil is real. I know it, because I've felt it. No one can talk you out of something you've actually felt, no matter how hard they try. But good is real, too. And I've felt that as well. So why one thing and not another? Why does this person die and this person doesn't? I don't know and, at least while I'm alive, I'm never going to know. But I know there's a God, and he has angels that help him deal with us down here, and this part of the story here isn't all there is. There's more to the story. I guess you could say that would be my answer."

I told him it sounded like a pretty good one.

Ten days after the accident at the Spanish Fork Bridge, there was an official presentation at the Spanish Fork Fire Department to honor Lily and all the people in her life and, especially, those who had been there to rescue her. Officers, doctors, firemen, ambulance drivers, nurses, EMTs . . . everyone who took part in saving Lily. Most brought presents. "It was a real party," Tyler said.

Jill had been at the party, but there had been so many people there that neither remembered actually meeting. But among the people Tyler met at the event that he did remember was Lily's biological dad.

"I talked to him, hugged him, cried with him," Tyler said. "He was real sincere, real genuine, real respectful. You could tell there was no way he didn't just love that child. You know, everyone talks about how he's a rough dude, how he had issues, how Jenny had issues. Me, I don't really judge people who've had issues because I've had some myself, and so has just about everyone I know."

I told Tyler I'd had some issues myself in the course of my life, that most of the people I knew also had issues of one sort or another. I also told him that this book was not going to be about people's issues. It was going to be about something else.

Tyler also got to hold Lily in his arms for a minute and look into her eyes. When he did, he told me, he had one of those strange moments of overlap—like when he'd come home and seen his family asleep in his bed and suddenly seen the Boren family lying there instead, superimposed over them. Now, for a moment, looking down into Lily's eyes, he had a flashback to the moment when he'd seen Jenny's face—her cruelly, brutally, irreversibly destroyed face.

But this time, something different happened. Something a

little like when, in the middle of the Boren horror, he had felt those kids at his legs. Looking into Lily's eyes, the ruined face of her mom transformed, and it was like he was meeting Jenny Groesbeck—the real, living Jenny Groesbeck—after all.

And she was telling him something. She was telling him, through the innocent eyes of the child in his arms that he had played such a big part in rescuing, what the Boren children, or the angels representing them, had told him, too.

It's okay.

Epilogue

Moments before the bomb went off I was standing by the sink, throwing up. I was sick from the smell of gasoline. I put water on my face. David put the string that was attached to the bomb around his wife's arm and walked to the back of the classroom to use the restroom. While I was standing at the sink I heard a voice say, "Matthew, go over by the window." I didn't think much of it, but I heard it again. "Matthew, go over by the window." Still I ignored the command. And then a third time, I heard the same voice say, "Matthew William! Go over by the window!" When I heard "Matthew William" I knew I was in trouble and I better do what I was told. So I went over to the window. I was only there long enough to sit on the windowsill and look outside for a second and then the bomb went off.

—MATTHEW WILLIAM BUCKLEY, COKEVILLE SURVIVOR,
WRITING TWENTY YEARS AFTER THE EVENT

Even though I was only eight at the time I still remember all the little details. Like the line of kids to the bathroom,

171

the smell of gasoline (which was making everyone sick), kids
vomiting in the sink, and the angels all around the room.
I knew they were angels because they were all white, and
brighter than the rest of the room.

—TAREESA COVERT, COKEVILLE SURVIVOR,

TWENTY YEARS AFTER THE INCIDENT

Iᶠ ᴛʜᴇʀᴇ ɪs a spiritual problem in our world today, it is not
that people don't have spiritual experiences. They have them
all the time—just as much as they did in medieval France, in
pre-Conquest America, or in the northwest deserts of aboriginal
Australia twenty thousand years ago.

If there is a spiritual problem in our
world today, it is not that people don't
have spiritual experiences.

And many of these include angels. In his book *The Sacred
History*, Mark Booth paints the broad picture:

An online survey conducted by the Bible Society and ICM
in the UK in 2010 reported that 31 percent believed in
angels, 29 percent believed in guardian angels and 5 percent
believed they had personally seen or heard an angel.
    In America the statistics are much higher. In 2008,
Time *magazine reported a survey showing that 69 percent*
of Americans believed in angels, 46 percent believed in

guardian angels and 32 percent claimed to have had a direct encounter with an angel.

"Mystical experiences are widespread," Rodney Stark, co-director of Baylor University's Institute for Studies of Religion, said in response to a question about the results of a study similar to the ones cited by Booth above. "This is the taboo subject in American religion. No one studies it, but there is a lot of it out there."

The problem is that we have lost the ability— and the courage—to "read" these experiences and to develop a truly common, truly across-all- borders way of speaking about them.

So the problem is not that we have lost the ability to experience the world beyond our materialistic prejudices, beyond our glass helmets. The problem is that we have lost the ability—and the courage—to "read" these experiences and to develop a truly common, truly across-all-borders way of speaking about them: the kind of language that two men waiting for a plane at an airport would use if they were talking about a football game happening on a screen overhead. These two men know the rules of the game in front of them. They know the players, they know the teams that are behind in the season so far and the teams that are ahead, and most likely they each have a different team that they're rooting for. When they fall into conversation about the game in front of them, they do so without awkwardness, without stiffness, without having to know anything about each other beyond the fact that each follows the game. They converse with an ease and swiftness that makes it seem as if they've known each other all their lives—even though they just started talking a few minutes before and probably won't see each other ever again.

Why can they do this? Because the game is common territory. One of the men might think one of the teams is better, or that one of the players is particularly likable or despicable. And the other man may disagree completely. It doesn't matter. In fact, it's often precisely these differences in opinion that make the conversation interesting.

In times past, the single most important common territory humans shared was their religious beliefs. To understate the matter, this is not the case anymore, and it has torn our world apart. Where is God? Does he exist at all? If he does exist, what sort of a fellow is he? Is he really even a "he" at all? Perhaps he's a "she" or an "it," or perhaps none of these pronouns are appropriate to use. Whatever or whoever God is, does he care about us? If he does, then why does he so often have such an odd way of showing it? What happens to us when we die? Will we understand more of God and what he's all about then, or will we simply cease to exist, and hence cease to understand anything?

We need to be jolted back onto that common field of concern about such matters. We need to return to a state of mind in which the spiritual world is seen to be as real as the ocean, and as full of different environments and different creatures. Recently, I was listening to a brilliant author hold forth on angels, then brush off Milton because, not being a Catholic, he was, in this author's mind, essentially not a Christian. That, in my opinion, is not the kind of mind-set we need right now. We need a mind-set that is tolerant of other faiths but aware as well that all those faiths, in their different ways and perhaps with greater and lesser degrees of accuracy, address a real place: the world above this one.

Angels are key figures in this return to a general, across-the-faiths respect for the spiritual world, because they are genuine beings that have manifested in genuine ways to sane, ordinary people whose lives have been changed forever by those encounters.

In this book we have been concerned with experiences that transcend philosophical argument, experiences that were so real to the people who lived through them that later, when those people got together to discuss them, no one had the slightest doubt that they had happened. We desperately need to hear about such events today. We have a critical need not for signs and wonders, because we already have them. What we need is the faculty to open our minds and accept them. We need events that demonstrate that the spiritual world is real, that it is populated, and that it is watched over by a God who cares about us.

> *We have a critical need not for signs and wonders, because we already have them. What we need is the faculty to open our minds and accept them. We need events that demonstrate that the spiritual world is real, that it is populated, and that it is watched over by a God who cares about us.*

At this point nothing else—nothing less—will do.
To tackle these issues, we do not need to be afraid of science.

Far from it. For at the cutting edge of the disciplines of both science and philosophy today, there lie the beginnings of a whole new style of looking at the world around us: one that exposes the rock-solid physical objects we encounter as not nearly so rock-solid after all, and the strange, hard-to-believe encounters with angelic beings that so many people report as not so nutty and impossible either. Experiences like Tyler's happen all the time. But they aren't spoken about, because the model of reality most of us were given in school and throughout our lives cannot accommodate them.

This has happened countless times before in history. Looking the other way is, simply, what humanity does with new experiences. Just a few hundred years ago, scientists in Europe refused to keep or examine meteors that were brought to them by people who had seen them fall out of the sky and strike the earth. Why? Because the scientists knew that rocks don't fall out of the sky. Just as they "know," today, that angelic beings cannot exist.

It's time for us to break our helmets—those helmets that feel, when we are wearing them, that they are not filtering anything out, but which are in fact filtering out a whole other dimension of existence. It's time to be done with the invisible glass that surrounds us and see the whole world, not just half of it.

Afterword

ONE DAY TYLER came home and Brittany presented him with a poem she'd written about Lily.

"She doesn't want it published or anything," Tyler told me. "It's just the kind of poem one mom might write for another mom who she feels for."

I read it and said I thought it was pretty good. I told Tyler I'd see if I could get it in the book.

"That's great," Tyler said. "She really didn't write it for that, but I'll bet she'd be tickled."

It's cold and dark but you are here,
your presence keeps me warm.
You do not look the same to me,
but I know that you're my mom.
You whisper to me softly—tell me it will be all right.
You smile as if you know it's true,
for you have seen the light.
You stayed there with me until they came,
the heroes dressed in blue.

Your voice guided them to me.
Yes, I know that it was you.
They got me out,
they kept me warm.
The docs worked on me for hours.
You knew it was time for you to go,
you'd done all that was in your power.
You gently kissed me on the cheek
and brushed my hair back softly.
You knew that your task was done,
but I was needed here.
Thank you Mom for being my angel,
I will miss you, but I know that you are near.

BY BRITTANY BEDDOES

Acknowledgments

Ptolemy Tompkins

At a pool where I swim in the summer, usually in the hours just before closing when most of the other members have gone home, I sometimes get to talking to whichever lifeguard is on duty, sitting in the chair over the pool like a god atop a throne, usually bored, with nothing to do but watch me swim back and forth.

Each year the pool hires a new company to look after it, so each year there is a new gaggle of lifeguards from the one before. At the beginning of last summer, when I was also at the beginning of writing this book, I struck up a conversation with one of the new lifeguards. I asked her how old she was—fifteen—and about her parents.

"My dad's dead," she said, matter-of-factly.

"Oh, I'm sorry," I said, feeling guilty for having brought the subject up and at the same time hating the weak ring of those standard words of condolence.

"It's okay," she said. "I don't mind talking about it."

"When did he die?" I asked.

179

"Just last year."

"How old was he?"

"Fifty-three."

My age. I swam around a little more, and the girl asked me what I did for a living—a reasonable question for an adult in a swimming pool at four o'clock on a Tuesday afternoon.

"I'm a writer. I write in the mornings but I usually run out of gas around three. Then I go to the gym or I come here."

"What kind of stuff do you write about?"

"Spiritual things. Actually, the most popular book I wrote, I did with someone else. It's called *Proof of Heaven*, about a surgeon who had an NDE."

"A what?"

"A near-death experience. Like, your body dies but then comes back to life, and you remember what happened in between."

The girl didn't say anything. At fifteen, she might not ever have heard the term *near-death experience*. I hadn't when I was her age. I figured I had probably said enough. But when I passed by again, I couldn't resist continuing the conversation. I asked if her family was religious.

"Not really," she said. "I mean, there was a funeral with a priest and everything, but no, not that much."

"Okay. So let me ask you a question. Your dad—he's gone from this world. His body is dead and buried, right?"

"Um . . . right," the girl said, probably starting to wonder who this person ready to ask such completely inappropriate questions was.

"So," I said, "what does that mean to you? Your dad was a

lot of things to you, right? He wasn't just a body with a skull and a brain. He was a whole vast and incredibly complex set of relations and meanings. Stuff that only you know, that only he knew—invisible stuff, but stuff that had a huge emotional weight for the both of you. Right?"

The girl, in her red lifeguard's uniform, shifted slightly in her seat above me. "Sure."

"So," I said, treading water down there in front of her, "where did all that go? Did it just evaporate, or is it still around somewhere, still in existence, even if you, if I, if no one can actually see it or feel it?"

"Oh," the girl said, as if she'd suddenly realized the obvious point I was making. "I know he's . . . around. It'll be like I get this little sense inside me, and I know he's there. He's still with me."

For the rest of the summer, while writing this book, I'd see that lifeguard up in her chair, and it would remind me of the seriousness of what I was writing about—that there wasn't a word in this book that I was putting together that was theoretical— and if there was such a word, I needed to take it out.

In addition to that lifeguard who played such a strange but valuable part in this book, I'd like to thank Tyler, Brittany, Jill, and the rest of the people of Spanish Fork and vicinity with whom I spoke. Their candor is responsible for whatever genuine life is to be found in these pages. I'd also like to thank my wife, Colleen, my stepdaughters Mara, Lulu, and Evie, Richard Smoley, Godfrey Cheshire, Mitch Horowitz, Bokara Legendre, Michael Baldwin, Bill Manning, Sonia, Ana, Elani, and Sister Cecilia, Ike and Carl at Nyack Vapes, my wonderful editor at

Howard Books, Beth Adams, both for her enthusiasm and for actually *editing the book*, something you don't always see these days, Katherine Sandell, Mia Crowley, Marla Jea, the book's extremely talented copy editor, who saved us from many an embarrassment, Jonathan Merkh, my sharp and ever-patient agent Art Klebanoff, Jennifer Gates and everyone at Zachary Shuster Harmsworth, Christina Johnstone and Sam Manning, Anna Sproul-Latimer, Richard Ryan, Karl Taro Greenfeld, Kate Farrell, Lisa "Free Dog" Snyder, and Archie, our Jack Russell terrier, who for a full summer put up with an owner who was all too stationary for his tastes.

· Tyler Beddoes

I first want to thank God for making this book happen. Without God giving me faith, courage, and comfort and opening my eyes to this world, it would not have been possible.

I want to thank my loving and gorgeous wife, Brittany, for being so supportive and helpful while I was spending a lot of time working on this book. Thank you to my two amazing kids, Gracie and Gunnar, who put a smile on my face every day! Thank you to my mom for always being there when I needed to talk and being so supportive and loving to me! I owe so much to you! Thank you, Dad, for being the best father someone could have asked for. Your example, support, and kindness haven't gone unnoticed, and it has made me stand a little taller to try to be more like you, and I am blessed for that! Thank you to my brother, Zack, for always pushing me harder and being there for me. You are such a great example and someone I really look up to and aspire to be. To my sister-in-law, Heidi, thank you for all your help, support, and kindness. Grandma Anna, I love you and thank you for always being there for me and our family. You are an amazing woman, and I love you! A big thank you to my Grandpa Donald for always pushing me to do my very best! Although you aren't with us today, I know you are in the heavens smiling down on all of us, and I know that you are proud!

Thank you to my in-laws, Shelly and Kirt, for being great and supportive to me. I love you both! Thank you to my father-in-law, Kenny, who had faith in me and was supportive of me from the very beginning. My brothers- and sisters-in-law Rachel, Jed, Emily, Jake, Kallysta, and Chase—thank you all! To the rest of my family, thank you: I couldn't have done this without you!! To my great friends and coworkers, thank you for all your support and kindness throughout this process. Thank you especially to Jason and Angie for your support, friendship, and kindness.

Thank you to the beautiful Lily and Jenny Groesbeck for really changing and giving me a new outlook on life. I am so very grateful to my agent, Jennifer Gates, for her awesome representation and for believing in my ideas for this book from the very beginning. This would not have been possible without you and everyone who was involved at Zachary Shuster Harmsworth. Thank you to Jonathan, Beth, and everyone at Howard Books and Simon & Schuster who had a hand in making this dream of mine become a reality.

Last but not least, I want to thank my coauthor, Ptolemy Tompkins. I have never met a greater man. Thank you so much for putting up with me and writing what I feel is an incredible book. You took my stories and experiences and truly put my exact feelings on paper, which wasn't easy to do. It was amazing working with such an intelligent and talented person, and I learned so much from you! Anyone else I failed to mention who helped along the way, offered advice, and was supportive of this book, THANK YOU!

Notes

1   *"Don't try to prove anything.":* Pierre Jovanovic, *An Inquiry into the Existence of Guardian Angels: A Journalist's Investigative Report* (New York: M. Evans & Company, 1997), 149. The quote is from an interview Jovanovic conducted with Elisabeth Kübler-Ross.

6   *"I picked one":* Howard Storm, *My Descent into Death: A Second Chance at Life* (New York: Harmony Books, 2005), p. 11.

7   *"church again!":* Ibid., p. 13.

15 *"From a certain point":* Franz Kafka, *The Zürau Aphorisms*, trans. Michael Hoffmann, ed. Roberto Calasso (New York: Schocken Books), p. 7, aphorism 5.

17 *"Ten years ago":* Meg Maxwell and Verena Tschudin, *Seeing the Invisible: Modern Religious and Other Transcendental Experiences* (London: Arkana), pp. 75–76.

31 *"Of Paradise, so late":* John Milton, *Paradise Lost*, ed. Alastair Fowler, 2nd ed. (Oxon: Routledge, 1997), bk. 12, lines 642–50.

33 *"Every angel is terrifying.":* Rainer Maria Rilke, *The Duino Elegies*, trans. Edward Snow (New York: North Point Press, 2001), p. 5, line 7. 000

38 *"Humankind cannot":* T. S. Eliot, "Burnt Norton," *Four Quartets* (New York: Mariner Books, 1968), p. 14, lines 42–43.

44 *"For beauty is nothing":* Rainer Maria Rilke, *The Duino Elegies*, trans. Edward Snow (New York: North Point Press, 2001), p. 5, lines 4–7.

47 *"I was a matron"*: Meg Maxwell and Verena Tschudin, *Seeing the Invisible*, pp. 137–38.

73 *"Excell thought the man"*: Hartt and Judene Wixom, *The Cokeville Miracle* (Springville, UT: Cedar Fort Publishing, 2015), 23. Originally published as *When Angels Intervene to Save the Children*, this remarkable book came back into print in 2015 to coincide with a film made about the event. (The book was adapted once before, for a 1994 TV movie starring Richard Thomas as David Young). Our quick retelling of the event does not do remote justice to the events of that day, and readers are encouraged not to miss the Wixoms' book. The couple had a child at Cokeville Elementary that day, and their account is not only extremely well written but, because of the Wixoms' intimate involvement in what occurred that day, one of the most convincing and moving accounts of angelic intervention ever written.

81 *"After the sudden death"*: Meg Maxwell and Verena Tschudin, *Seeing the Invisible*, pp. 71–72.

103 *"Lying on her bed"*: Mark Fox, *Spiritual Encounters with Unusual Light Phenomena: Lightforms* (Cardiff: University of Wales Press, 2008), 45. Fox is citing Cherie Sutherland's *In the Company of Angels: Welcoming Angels into Your Life* (Dublin: Gill & Macmillan, 2001), p. 45.

105 *"I remember hearing the doctors"*: Pierre Jovanovic, *An Inquiry into the Existence of Guardian Angels,* 309–10. Jovanovic, a French reporter disinclined to believe in or be interested in angels, had his mind changed after an inexplicable force moved him out of the way of a bullet, saving his life. His *Inquiry* is a smart, funny, endlessly entertaining and entirely believable journey through the world of guardian angels, and easily one of the most valuable contemporary books on the subject of angels, period. Those interested in the kind of story recounted here will find many, many more in the book's pages.

110 *"One night in October"*: Pierre Jovanovic, *An Inquiry into the Existence of Guardian Angels,* p. 109.

114   *"While I'm staring at the instruments"*: Rosemary Ellen Guilley, *The Encyclopedia of Angels*, 2nd ed. (New York: Facts on File/Visionary Living), 216–17. All of the Lindbergh material quoted here came from Guilley's *Encyclopedia*, the first edition of which I raided constantly during my tenure at *Angels on Earth*. Along with Gustav Davidson's (more academic but also more stuffy) *Dictionary of Angels*, Guilley's *Encyclopedia* is *the* source for information on all aspects of angels, from the thoughts of the Church Fathers all the way on up to the kaleidoscopic New Age heterodoxies of today.

115   *"I could not feel lonely"*: Theodora Ward, *Of Men and Angels: A Personal Study of a Persisting Symbol in Western Culture* (New York: Viking Press, 1969), 213. If Rosemary Ellen Guilley's *Encyclopedia* is the most comprehensive contemporary source for information on angels, Theodora Ward's book, though published almost fifty years ago, is still probably the best all-around introduction to what angels are or might be, and what they have meant to people down through the centuries. In a world flooded with not-so-great books about angels, it is a shame that this one is currently out of print.

127   *"My dear brothers"*: Charles Baudelaire, from the short story "Le Joueur généreux," first published in France in 1864.

129   *"The Siren Call"*: Joe Fisher, *The Siren Call of Hungry Ghosts* (New York: Paraview Press, 2001). For all its darkness and frequent naiveté, *The Siren Call of Hungry Ghosts* remains one of the truly essential books for anyone interested in exploring just how real, and dangerous, the world of spirit communication as practiced by various New Age and other groups these days can be.

139   *"All of us"*: Herman Melville, *Typee, Omoo, Mardi* (New York: Library of America, 1982), p. 662.

147   *"Fifteen years ago"*: Quoted in Robert Sardello, *The Angels* (New York: Continuum, 2001), p. 23.

159   *"Perhaps all the dragons"*: Rainer Maria Rilke, *Letters to a Young*

Poet, trans. M. D. Herter Norton, rev. ed. (New York: W. W. Norton & Company, 1993), p. 52.

173   *"Moments before the bomb went off": Witness to Miracles: Remembering the Cokeville Elementary School Bombing* (Greybull, WY: Pronghorn Press, 2006), p. 109.

173   *"Even though I was only eight":* Ibid., p. 87.

About the Authors

PTOLEMY TOMPKINS is the author of seven books, including *The Divine Life of Animals* and *The Modern Book of the Dead*. In 2012, he collaborated with Dr. Eben Alexander on the phenomenal worldwide bestseller *Proof of Heaven*, and coauthored its sequel, *The Map of Heaven*, as well. For just under ten years he was an editor and writer at *Guideposts* and *Angels on Earth* magazines. His writing has appeared in numerous other magazines as well, including *The New York Times Magazine*, *Harper's*, and

Time. He appears in the 2014 film *Monk with a Camera*, which chronicles the life of his stepbrother Nicholas Vreeland, the first Westerner to become abbot of a Tibetan Buddhist monastery. He is also the author of *The Beaten Path*, a book which chronicles his adventures growing up with a Buddhist for a stepbrother, and explores the differences between Buddhism and Christianity. He lives in Nyack, New York, with his wife, Colleen, and two of his three stepdaughters.

TYLER BEDDOES was born in Provo, Utah. He studied criminal justice and journalism at Utah Valley University. He joined the Spanish Fork Police Department in Spanish Fork, Utah, in 2006. While a member of the police department he was awarded an exemplary service award for his part in investigating a quadruple homicide committed by Joshua Boren in January 2014. He was also recognized by the mayor of Spanish Fork and the United States Congress for his involvement in the miraculous rescue of Lily Groesbeck from the Spanish Fork River on the morning of March 7, 2015. He currently resides in Elk Ridge, Utah, with his wife, Brittany, and their two children, Gracie and Gunnar.